Books by Corliss Lamont

The Philosophy of Humanism, Seventh edition, Continuum, New York, NY, 1990.

The Illusion of Immortality, Fifth edition, Continuum, New York, NY, 1990.

Freedom of Choice Affirmed, Third edition, Continuum, New York, NY, 1990.

Freedom Is As Freedom Does: Civil Liberties in America, Fourth edition, Continuum, New York, NY, 1990.

Yes To Life: Memoirs of Corliss Lamont, Continuum, New York, NY, 1990.

Remembering John Masefield, Continuum, New York, NY, 1990.

A Lifetime of Dissent, Prometheus Books, 700 East Amherst St., Buffalo, NY, 14215, 1988.

Voice in the Wilderness: Collected Essays of Fifty Years, Prometheus Books, 700 East Amherst St., Buffalo, NY, 14215, 1974.

The Independent Mind, Horizon Press, New York, NY, 1951.

The Peoples of the Soviet Union, Harcourt, Brace & Co., New York, NY, 1946.

Russia Day by Day (Co-author with Margaret I. Lamont), Covici-Friede, New York, 1933.

Soviet Civilization, Second edition, Philosophical Library, New York, NY, 1952, 1955.

You Might Like Socialism, Modern Age Books, New York, NY, 1939.

Lover's Credo: Poems of Love, William L. Bauhan, Dublin, NH, 03444.

A Humanist Wedding Service, Prometheus Books, 700 East Amherst St., Buffalo, NY, 14215, 1970.

A Humanist Funeral Service, Prometheus Books, 700 East Amherst St., Buffalo, NY, 14215, 1977.

(Continued on last page of book)

FREEDOM OF CHOICE AFFIRMED

CORLISS LAMONT

FREEDOM OF CHOICE AFFIRMED

HALF-MOON FOUNDATION, INC.

The Half-Moon Foundation was formed to promote enduring international peace, support for the United Nations, the conservation of our country's natural environment, and to safeguard and extend civil liberties as guaranteed under the Constitution and the Bill of Rights.

A Frederick Ungar Book
CONTINUUM • NEW YORK

v

To
HELEN LAMB LAMONT

1990

The Continuum Publishing Company
370 Lexington Avenue
New York, NY 10017

Third Edition

Printed in the United States of America

Library of Congress Catalog Card No. 67-27793
ISBN 0-8264-0476-6

Cover: Detail of "The Thinker" (Le Penseur) by Auguste Rodin.
Reprinted with permission of The Fine Arts Museums of San Francisco,
Gift of Alma de Bretteville Spreckels. Phtograph by Joe Schopplein.

Contents

Preface to the Third Edition

Since the publication of the second edition of *Freedom of Choice Affirmed* in 1967 I have made an important change in my position on freedom of choice. On page 169 of the second edition I state: "There is a strong, immediate, commonsense intuition in practically all human beings that we possess true freedom in choosing between real alternatives." I now say that the intuition referred to governs the situation. In other words, free choice is an innate, inborn, natural power of human beings that enables them to state "I could have chosen otherwise," after any decision goes into effect. No arguments can negate this final conclusion.

Corliss Lamont

New York City
April, 1990

Preface to the Third Edition

Preface

I have been thinking about the question of freedom of choice and determinism for more than forty years, ever since I began my professional study of philosophy at Columbia University in 1926. During these four decades I have done a vast amount of reading on this issue, accumulated extensive notes, participated in private discussions and public debates, and made every effort to arrive at intelligent and objective conclusions. Admittedly, the problem is one of the most difficult and complex in the entire range of philosophy.

At the outset I must make clear that since I adhere to the philosophy of naturalistic Humanism, I cannot, in trying to establish the existence of free choice, accept any dualistic device of a supernatural or transcendental soul that intervenes in or supersedes the natural sequences of cause and effect. In the humanist view, mind, personality and all other human attributes belong completely to this world and the realm of Nature.

I have stressed the phrase "freedom of choice" both

because of the theological connotations and confusions associated with the term "free will" and because there is nothing identifiable as "the will" which is responsible for a man's choices. It is the whole personality that does the choosing and it is the whole personality that carries out the actions entailed in choice.

In my studies concerning free choice I have been especially indebted to Dr. Mortimer J. Adler's two-volume compendium, *The Idea of Freedom;* to Sir Isaiah Berlin's *Historical Inevitability;* to Professor Milič Čapek of Boston University for his *The Philosophical Impact of Contemporary Physics* and his article "The Doctrine of Necessity Re-Examined"; to Professor Charles Hartshorne of the University of Texas for his *The Logic of Perfection;* and to Sterling P. Lamprecht, Professor of Philosophy Emeritus at Amherst College, for his books *Nature and History* and *The Metaphysics of Naturalism.* I have also drawn upon the discussion of freedom of choice in my own volume, *The Philosophy of Humanism.*

In *Freedom of Choice Affirmed* I have tried to write a book that will not only prove useful to professional philosophers, especially in college teaching, but that also can be understood by the average reader. Hence I have avoided as far as possible both technical terminologies and technical discussions. Philosophy is hard enough to comprehend without wrapping it up in semantic complexities that bewilder the normal mind.

Corliss Lamont

New York City
July 1, 1967

The Continuing Controversy

Since the publication of *Freedom of Choice Affirmed* in the fall of 1967, the great debate in philosophic circles over the question of free choice and determinism has continued unabated. Books, articles, addresses, symposiums and colloquiums on this issue are a marked phenomenon of the times. There can be no doubt that the problem of free will is a matter of prime concern not only to contemporary philosophers but also to economists, historians, scientists and the educated mind in general.

During the past two years I have been engaged in voluminous correspondence about my book and the entire subject of freedom of choice. When in my study I mentioned certain eminent philosophers who have been determinists, I included Bertrand Russell (see page 56). Almost a year later, in an exchange of letters with Lord Russell, I discovered that the generally held view of him as a determinist was mistaken.

Dr. Erich Fromm put me on the trail when he stated in a symposium, *Bertrand Russell: Philosopher of the Century*

(1967): "He [Russell] is not a determinist who claims that the historical future is already determined; he is an 'alternativist' who sees that what is determined are certain limited and ascertainable alternatives." I was intrigued by Fromm's new word"alternativist"for one who believes in free will.

I wrote to Russell, quoting Fromm's comment, and added: "Now this fits in precisely with my own viewpoint. Opposing the extremes to which Sartre goes on this question, I claim that free choice is *always* limited by one's heredity, environment, economic circumstances and so on. Those are the deterministic elements in the picture. But beyond them, though established by them, are real alternatives among which a man can choose. That is where free choice comes in.

"You have usually been classified as a determinist," I went on. "But if Fromm's remarks are correct, as well as my interpretation of them, you are by no means a total determinist and have been misunderstood."

Russell promptly replied: "I am in broad agreement with what you say about the free will question. Anything one says on this is sure to be wrong! It is difficult to find a form of words, and the difficulty is due to linguistic problems. There are no laws of nature that make the future certain. Any scientific investigator would always have to assume determinism as a working hypothesis, without complete belief or complete denial. *I cannot be described as a determinist,* and my views are closer to yours than to Sartre's." [My italics. — C.L.]

Another outstanding philosopher commonly thought to have been a determinist is George Santayana. However, in *Dominations and Powers* (1951), the last of his books published while he was alive, Santayana comes around to a free choice position. He offers a rather unusual view of free will, but makes plain that he thinks it exists. He writes (pages 53–54):

"I think that intense scrutiny of immediate experience does yield an intuition of a truth; not at all, however, of the truth about the ground or origin of human decisions, but about the *inadequacy* of the conscious arguments crowding and disputing in the mind to cause or justify the decisions taken. With this comes also the intuition of a positive truth, that beneath that loud forum of sophistical pleadings there is a silent judge, the *self*, that decides according to its free will, contingently and inexplicably. For the close texture of events in nature is what it is by chance; yet what it is by chance determines, according to the occasion offered, what it shall do by nature.

"The affinities of this self are far more constant and certain than the passing passions or influences that may absorb conscious attention. Therefore the self can check its reasoning fancy; it can repel sensuous suggestions; it can seek dangerous adventures apparently without reason; it can recover its freedom, and reverse its habits and opinions. Moreover, this hidden self is, like every other center or kind of movement in nature, perfectly contingent in being groundlessly determinate; and to this profound characteristic of all existence self-consciousness bears witness in the conviction that a man is the author of his actions, and that his actions are free."

Santayana's emphasis on the contingent or chance leads me to say that my own insistence in *Freedom of Choice Af-*

firmed on the existence of contingency has been seriously misunderstood. I do not mean that our choices stem from pure chance, but that chance as a cosmic correlative of necessity knocks out the argument for total determinism and opens the way for free choice without guaranteeing its existence. Contingency was always present in the universe and therefore operative long before life and man evolved upon this planet.

Contingency affects free will specifically by ensuring that when a man is considering various alternatives or potentialities, there is *indeterminacy* as to which he will choose. His selection of one particular alternative has not been foreordained, as the determinist philosophy claims. The individual, deliberating about alternatives and trying to foresee the probable consequences of each, then makes a decision. In putting it into effect, he often utilizes the determinism inherent in some scientific law or manmade machine.

The Humanist (March/April 1968) prints a challenging review of *Freedom of Choice Affirmed* by Professor of Philosophy Dale Riepe of the State University of New York at Buffalo. Commenting on my case for the existence of free choice, Riepe states: "Lamont does provide proofs, but commonly they turn out to be examples of his initial intuition of freedom of which 'contingency' is a part." But I maintain that my "proofs" or arguments cannot be reduced to mere intuition and that it is deliberative reason that shows them to be sound. I do not think that my immediate intuition of free choice includes a direct awareness of contingency, necessity and potentiality. These ideas can be established as true only through a sophisticated process of observation and deduction.

Riepe also writes: "Potentiality . . . outside of the context of determinacy has no meaning. To know what has potentiality one must know the antecedent and determining events." Of course. But the deterministic aspect of potentiality does not exhaust its meaning. As Dr. Fromm noted, "What is determined are certain limited and ascertainable alternatives." Such alternatives or potentialities when confronted by an individual are contingent in relation to his choosing; and that contingency is an essential factor in enabling him to make a free choice.

The idea of freedom of choice is, according to Riepe, "vague and illusive." Most definitions of free choice do fit this characterization. The concept becomes clearer when we note that it means, among other things, that a person looking back on a decision can say with truth: "I could have chosen otherwise, even under the same circumstances." If I could not have decided otherwise, then I had only the power to choose the alternative I chose; and in that case I did not have free will.

I agree with Riepe that it is difficult to ascertain objectively the psychological and moral consequences of belief in universal, all-inclusive determinism. Here I must stress that since the power of free choice is, in my opinion, an inborn human characteristic—as innate as the faculty of thinking—it is all but impossible for an individual to carry through consistently the implications of determinism in the sum total of his actions. For example, militant radicals and Marxists may espouse economic determinism, but usually act as if the thesis of free will were true. Theoretical determinists are like theoretical solipsists in that they are unable to practice what they preach.

A stern Calvinist preacher was traveling on a Mississippi River steamboat in the early days. As Mark Twain recounts in *Life on the Mississippi*, the steamboat captains liked to race against each other, sometimes with disastrous results to their craft and passengers. When the boat carrying the Reverend started to race, he nervously asked the captain to put him ashore "at the first opportunity." "But," said the captain, "I thought you believed that through the will of God everything that happens is bound to happen just that way."

"Yes," the preacher replied, "but I don't have to stay around till it happens."

—Corliss Lamont

New York City
June 1, 1969

PART ONE

1
The Perennial Debate

The "labyrinthine dispute" over freedom of choice and determinism has been one of the great perennial issues in Western philosophy ever since the intellectual flowering of ancient Greece from the sixth to the fourth centuries B.C. Referring to several of the pre-Socratic philosophers, Plutarch writes: "Thales says that necessity is omnipotent, and that it exerciseth an empire over every thing. Pythagoras, that the world is invested by necessity. Parmenides and Democritus, that there is nothing in the world but what is necessarily, and that this same necessity is otherwise called fate, justice, providence, and the architect of the world." [1]

Of the thinkers cited by Plutarch, Democritus (c. 480-c. 370 B.C.), a complete determinist and progenitor of the atomic theory verified some two millennia later, gave the clearest formulation of determinism. He states: "The causes of things now coming into being . . . have no be-

13

ginning; but from infinite time back, all things that were and are and will be are foreordained by necessity." [2] A century or so later Epicurus took over much of Democritus' materialism, but insisted that chance deviations occurred in the swirl of the atoms, thus breaking the monopoly of determinism and making room for free will.

Epicurus, like Democritus, wanted to liberate men from the fear of supernatural gods and their arbitrary interference in human affairs. Even more to be deplored, according to Epicurus, was the conception of universal necessity enunciated by Democritus. "It were better," contends Epicurus, "to follow the myths about the gods than to become a slave to the 'destiny' of the natural philosophers: for the former suggests a hope of placating the gods by worship, whereas the latter involves a necessity which knows no placation." [3]

In the first century B.C., Lucretius, the great philosopher poet of ancient Rome, adopted the system of Epicurus and describes in his masterly work, *On the Nature of Things*, the "swerve" of the atoms that makes freedom of choice possible:

This truth besides I fain would have thee learn
Ere thou proceed: when downwards through the void,
Straight on by force of their own weight, are borne
The primal bodies, quite at random times
And random places, some will push aside
A little space, yet only just so much
As thou mightst call the slightest change of trend.
Were they not wont to swerve, then must they all

Like drops of rain straight down through space profound
Forever fall, nor could there e'er arise
A single meeting, or a single blow
Among the first beginnings; so in all
The realm of nature naught would come to birth. . . .

Dost not, then, see by now that though ofttimes
A force without doth drive men on, and e'en
Against their will doth thrust them headlong, still
There doth remain a something in our breast
Which hath the power to hamper and to thwart—
Something at whose behest our matter's store
May be at times constrained to turn its course
Now here, now there, throughout the limbs, or now,
Spurred headlong forward, feel the curb and rein
And once again be brought to stand at rest? [4]

It is not my intention in this book to discuss in depth
or even to summarize the opinions of the outstanding philosophers concerning freedom of choice and determinism.
Suffice it to say that in the intervening 2,000 years since
Lucretius, every philosopher of note has taken part in this
age-long controversy as to whether a man is a puppet of
necessity and a toy of circumstance, or the captain of his
soul and, within limits, the master of his fate.

In 1884 William James, one of the best known ex-
ponents of free choice, wrote: "A common opinion prevails
that the juice has ages ago been pressed out of the free-will
controversy, and that no new champion can do more than
warm up stale arguments which every one has heard. This is
a radical mistake. I know of no subject less worn out, or in

which inventive genius has a better chance of breaking open new ground—not, perhaps, of forcing a conclusion or of coercing assent, but of deepening our sense of what the issue between the two parties really is, of what the ideas of fate and of free-will imply." [5]

Today, more than eighty years after James's statement, the situation remains much the same. The controversy over freedom of choice is sharp and lively both in America and in Europe, where Jean-Paul Sartre and Existentialism have brought the question to the fore since the end of World War II. In the United States and England, articles, books, symposia and radio forums continue to debate the issue. Dr. John David Mabbott, President of St. John's College, Oxford, phrases the problem in terms of a great philosophical drama: "Could it be possible . . . that the behavior of a single species on a minor planet in one of the countless solar systems should escape a type of determination which had been found to apply to the smallest particles of matter and the largest and most distant heavenly bodies?" [6] Historian Arnold Toynbee suggests that free choice is an undependable "joker" Nature has inserted into the psychosomatic pack of cards that constitutes a human being.

There are, of course, many different kinds of freedom: academic, cultural, economic, political, religious, freedom of speech and other freedoms. However, it is *freedom of choice* that I am concentrating on in this book, the freedom that is the most fundamental of all, underlying all other human freedoms.

Freedom of choice (free will), whose adherents are often called *libertarians*, means that a man who consciously comes to a decision between two or more genuine alternatives is free to do so and is not completely determined by his heredity, education, economic circumstances and past history as an individual. While a person's choices are always conditioned and limited to a marked extent by such factors and by the situation that currently faces him, he possesses a decisive element of freedom in determining whether to do this or that. Free choice, then, goes beyond the liberty from external constraint or compulsion which many philosophers have defined as true freedom.

Determinism, on the other hand, is the view that all events upon this earth and in the universe, including human choices both trivial and important, are governed by rigid causal sequences coming down from past to present—antecedent causes that necessitate a specific choice, and rule out any other. According to this theory, the causes that determine the destiny of men work through inheritance in combination with the potent pressures of society and the physical environment. The determinist standpoint is well summed up in the words, "Whatever is, was to be."

Mechanism and *necessity* are useful synonyms for determinism. *Fatalism* in the broad philosophic sense is equivalent to determinism, but has a somewhat more passive connotation. The fatalist is far more inclined than the determinist to lean back and let the world take its course. In his essay "On Fate" Cicero gives a classic example of fatalism: " 'If it is fated for you to recover from this illness, you will recover whether you call in a doctor or do not; similarly, if it is fated for you not to recover from this illness, you will not recover whether you call in a doctor or do not;

and either your recovery or non-recovery is fated; therefore there is no point in calling in a doctor.' This mode of arguing is rightly called 'idle' and indolent, because the same train of reasoning will lead to the entire abolition of action from life." [7]

To cite William James again, determinism "professes that those parts of the universe already laid down absolutely appoint and decree what the other parts shall be. The future has no ambiguous possibilities hidden in its womb: the part we call the present is compatible with only one totality. Any other future complement than the one fixed from eternity is impossible. The whole is in each and every part, and welds it with the rest into an absolute unity, an iron block, in which there can be no equivocation or shadow of turning." [8]

A few philosophers have maintained that the unceasing dispute over free will is simply a matter of semantics. Thus David Hume in his *Enquiry Concerning Human Understanding* (1748) asserts: "I hope, therefore, to make it appear that all men have ever agreed in the doctrine both of necessity and of liberty, according to any reasonable sense, which can be put on these terms; and that the whole controversy has hitherto turned merely upon words." [9] John Stuart Mill in the nineteenth century and Moritz Schlick in the twentieth take a position similar to Hume's. Professor Schlick, one of the founders of the Vienna Circle of logical positivists, calls the question of freedom of choice a "pseudo-problem." I reject the reasoning of these three thinkers.

The elusive issue of free choice and determinism has

traditionally been just as important in religion as philosophy. This is clearly the case as regards Buddhism and Hinduism, in both of which the law of *karma* deterministically settles the status of each individual in his successive reincarnations; in Mohammedanism, which from its inception has stressed its founder's doctrine of preordained destiny or *Kismet;* and in Christianity, in which both Catholic and Protestant theologians and churchmen have wrestled perpetually with the theory of divine predestination in relation to free will.

At the height of the Renaissance the great Erasmus stated: "Among the many difficulties encountered in Holy Scripture—and there are many of them—none presents a more perplexed labyrinth than the problem of the freedom of the will. In ancient and more recent times philosophers and theologians have been vexed by it to an astonishing degree, but, as it seems to me, with more exertion than success on their part." [10]

The debate on this theme was going strong as far back as the fourth and fifth centuries A.D. when St. Augustine, as the defender of predestination, waged ecclesiastical war against the heresies of a British monk, Pelagius, who upheld the doctrine of free will and man's responsibility for his own salvation. In the modern era the two outstanding figures of the Protestant Reformation, Martin Luther and John Calvin, firmly upheld theological determinism. In one of the historic intellectual duels on the question of free choice, Erasmus made a spirited attack on Luther in *A Diatribe or Sermon Concerning Free Will* (1524). Luther returned blow for blow in his philippic, *The Enslaved Will*

(1525). Characteristically, Luther declared that "God foreknows nothing contingently, but . . . foresees, purposes and does all things according to His immutable, eternal and infallible will. This thunderbolt throws free will flat and utterly dashes it to pieces." [11]

Arguing similarly from God's omnipotence and omniscience, including his foreknowledge of future events, the Calvinists carried on the tradition of religious determinism and developed an especially stern doctrine of predestination that regarded men as the puppets of a vengeful God. In colonial America the celebrated preacher and theologian, Jonathan Edwards, was the chief proponent of this theory; and his fiery sermons dwelt vividly on the terrors of immortality for those foredoomed to eternal damnation, including new-born infants who died after a few days. In harsh language Edwards warned: "The God that holds you over the pit of hell, much as one holds a spider, or some loathsome insect, over the fire, abhors you, and is dreadfully provoked: his wrath towards you burns like fire. . . . You are ten thousand times more abominable in his eyes than the most hateful venomous serpent is in ours. . . . There will be no end to this exquisite horrible misery." [12]

Edwards waged unremitting battle against the free-will heresy of Jacobus Arminius and the Arminians and wrote one of the great classics against the doctrine of free choice. He gave it the formidable title, *A Careful and Strict Enquiry into the Modern Prevailing Notions of that Freedom of Will Which is Supposed to be Essential to Moral Agency, Virtue and Vice, Reward and Punishment,*

Praise and Blame (1754). The familiar "There but for the grace of God go I" is a typical Calvinist sentiment.*

As time went on, however, Calvinist and Lutheran dogmas on free will moderated, and Protestant denominations in general adopted views on the issue similar to those of the Arminians. The Roman Catholic Church never accepted the doctrine of predestination preached by St. Augustine. Early in its history it committed itself to a definite free-will position, which was later developed and clarified by St. Thomas Aquinas in the thirteenth century and by various Church Councils. Today, virtually all Christian sects uphold some concept of freedom of choice, although in my judgment none of them has succeeded in making it consistent with the idea of an almighty and omniscient God.

It is worth noting that one group of Baptists in North Carolina who wished to stress freedom of choice broke away from the orthodox Baptist Church in 1727 and established the Free Will Baptists. Precisely a hundred years later, in 1827, a General Conference of Free Will Baptists was organized. This organization gave way in 1935 to the National Association of Free Will Baptists. The Free Will Baptist Church has its headquarters in Nashville, Tennessee and had attained by 1966 a membership of 255,000.

The Free Will Baptists hold that "God has endowed man with the power of free choice, and governs him by moral laws and motives; and this power of free choice is the

---

* The story has it that a Calvinist met a Methodist on his way to worship on a Sunday morning and remarked, "You were fore-ordained to go to church today." To which the Methodist replied, "Is that so?" and turned around and went home.

exact measure of man's responsibility. All events are present with God from everlasting to everlasting; but His knowledge of them does not in any sense cause them, nor does He decree all events which He knows will occur." [13]

Theological determinism has also acted as a catalyst in the controversy over the so-called "problem of evil": How can an omnipotent and totally good God, who absolutely controls everything that goes on in the universe, permit all the evil, pain, misery, violence and bloodshed that have afflicted the human race since it first appeared upon this earth? Logically, this problem of evil is insoluble, and God is transformed into a devil incarnate, unless man has true freedom of choice and therefore moral responsibility for a large measure of the ills that plague him.

Literature down the ages has also been much concerned with determinism and freedom, starting with the ancient Greek dramatists and their treatment of Fate. Perhaps the most memorable rendering of this theme was that of Sophocles in his tragedy, *Oedipus Rex*. However, in this brief review I am concentrating on writers of the nineteenth and twentieth centuries, and am presenting some highlights in their discussion of our problem.

In his novel, *The Bridge of San Luis Rey*, Thornton Wilder weaves into the story a variation on theological determinism. When five Peruvians crossing a rope bridge near Lima are hurled to their death as it suddenly breaks at noon on July 20, 1714, Brother Juniper, a Franciscan monk, becomes convinced that supernatural causes were at work. By searching into the details of the victims' lives, Brother Juniper tries to demonstrate that it was God's plan for them all to be on the bridge at the fatal moment. He sees in the accident a divine intent to have "the wicked visited by destruction and the good called early to Heaven. He thought he saw pride and wealth confounded as an object lesson to the world, and he thought he saw humility crowned and rewarded for the edification of the city." [14] His extensive researches and pious conclusions Brother Juniper put into an enormous book. The result was that the authorities soon burned both book and author in the public square.

In Leo Tolstoy's *War and Peace*, the Second Epilogue gives an outstanding discussion of the theme of freedom and determinism. In this lively essay Tolstoy comes out on the side of universal necessity. "If the will of every man were free," he argues, "that is, if each man could act as he pleased, all history would be a series of disconnected incidents. If in a thousand years even one man in a million could act freely, that is, as he chose, it is evident that one single free act of that man's in violation of the laws governing human action would destroy the possibility of the existence of any laws for the whole of humanity." [15]

In *A Mummer's Tale* by Anatole France, Dr. Socrates upholds the determinist viewpoint when he urges that M. Chevalier was not to be blamed for his suicide, because it was preordained from eternity. Says the eloquent Dr. Socrates:

"To call upon a poor wretch to answer for his actions! Why, even when the solar system was still no more than a pale nebula, forming, in the ether, a fragile halo, whose circumference was a thousand times greater than the orbit of Neptune, we had all of us, for ages past, been fully conditioned, determined and irrevocably destined, and your responsibility, my responsibility, Chevalier's and that of all men, had been, not mitigated, but abolished beforehand. All our movements, the result of previous movements of matter, are subject to the laws which govern the cosmic forces, and the human mechanism is merely a particular instance of the universal mechanism." [16]

In Herman Melville's *Moby Dick,* Captain Ahab feels that some imperious destiny is driving him on in his relentless, fatal pursuit of the Great White Whale. "What is it," Ahab cries, "what nameless, inscrutable, unearthly thing is it; what cozening, hidden lord and master, and cruel remorseless emperor commands me; that against all natural lovings and longings, I so keep pushing, and crowding, and jamming myself on all the time; recklessly making me ready to do what in my own proper, natural heart, I durst not so much as dare? Is Ahab, Ahab? Is it I, God, or who, that lifts this arm? But if the great sun move not of himself; but is an errand-boy in heaven; nor one single star can revolve, but by some invisible power; how then can this one small heart beat; this one small brain think thoughts; unless God does that beating, does that thinking, does that living, and not I? . . .

"By heaven, man, we are turned round and round in this world, like yonder windlass, and Fate is the handspike. And all the time, lo! that smiling sky, and this unsounded sea! . . . This whole act's immutably decreed. 'Twas rehearsed by thee and me a billion years before this ocean rolled. Fool! I am the Fates' lieutenant; I act under orders." [17]

Turning to drama and poetry, we find Cassius in Shakespeare's *Julius Caesar* declining to accept the determinism implicit in astrology:*

> Men at some time are masters of their fates:
> The fault, dear Brutus, is not in our stars,
> But in ourselves that we are underlings. . . .[18]

Edmund in *King Lear* is even more scornful of astrology:

> This is the excellent foppery of the world, that, when we are sick in fortune—often the surfeit of our own behaviour—we make guilty of our disasters the sun, the moon, and the stars: as if we were villains by necessity, fools by heavenly compulsion, knaves, thieves and treachers by spherical predominance, drunkards, liars and adulterers by an enforced obedience of planetary influence; and all that we are evil in, by a divine thrusting on: an admirable evasion of whoremaster man, to lay his goatish disposition to the charge of a star! My father compounded with my mother under the

* In the ancient world there was a widespread belief in astrology, and this pseudo-science flourished in Europe as late as the seventeenth century. Today it still has a large following, particularly in Oriental countries. Even in the United States, astrology claims to have several million devotees. At one time it entered into my own life because for several years I was confused with a practicing astrologer, Mr. C. W. Lemont, who like myself lived on Riverside Drive in New York City.

dragon's tail, and my nativity was under *ursa major*. 'Sfoot! I should have been that I am had the maidenliest star in the firmament twinkled at my bastardizing.[19]

A masterpiece of poetically rendered determinism appears in Edward Fitzgerald's *The Rubáiyát of Omar Khayyám:*

We are no other than a moving row
Of Magic Shadow-shapes that come and go
Round with the Sun-illumined Lantern held
In Midnight by the Master of the Show;

But helpless Pieces of the Game He plays
Upon this Chequer-board of Nights and Days;
Hither and thither moves, and checks, and slays,
And one by one back in the Closet lays. . . .

The Moving Finger writes; and, having writ,
Moves on: nor all your Piety nor Wit
Shall lure it back to cancel half a Line,
Nor all your Tears wash out a Word of it.

And that inverted Bowl they call the Sky,
Whereunder crawling cooped we live and die,
Lift not your hands to *It* for help—for It
Impotently moves as you or I.

With Earth's first Clay They did the Last Man knead,
And there of the Last Harvest sowed the Seed:
And the first Morning of Creation wrote
What the Last Dawn of Reckoning shall read.

The Rubáiyát poses the same conundrum that perennially perplexed the Christian theologians:

> O Thou, who didst with Pitfall and with Gin
> Beset the Road I was to wander in,
> Thou wilt not with Predestined Evil round
> Enmesh, and then impute my Fall to Sin!

Thomas Hardy's lines in his great poem, *The Dynasts*, are reminiscent of *The Rubáiyát:*

> The Immanent, that urgeth all,
> Rules what may or may not befall!
>
> Ere systemed suns were globed and lit
> The slaughters of the race were writ.
>
> And wasting wars, by land and sea,
> Fixed, like all else, immutably! . . .[20]
>
> Why doth IT so and so, and ever so,
> This viewless, voiceless Turner of the Wheel? . . .[21]
>
> We are but thistle-globes on heaven's high gales,
> And whither blown, or when, or how, or why,
> Can choose us not at all! [22]

With unflinching consistency, Hardy also presents a sombre and deterministic view in his novels, in which heartbreak and unhappiness are major themes. For him humanity is doomed to permanent frustration and tragedy. His profound pessimism seems to be bound up with the conviction that an iron necessity rules mankind and the universe.*

* Cf. pp. 153-54.

John Masefield in an eloquent sonnet harks back to the ancient predilection for astrology, and protests against determinism as applied to man:

If all be governed by the moving stars,
If passing planets bring events to be,
Searing the face of Time with bloody scars,
Drawing men's souls even as the moon the sea,
If as they pass they make a current pass
Across man's life and heap it to a tide,
We are but pawns, ignobler than the grass
Cropped by the beast and crunched and tossed aside.
Is all this beauty that doth inhabit heaven
Train of a planet's fire? Is all this lust
A chymic means by warring stars contriven
To bring the violets out of Caesar's dust?
Better be grass, or in some hedge unknown
The spilling rose whose beauty is its own.[23]

A philosophy of determinism is undoubtedly congenial to a considerable number of persons because it seems to relieve them of exertion in the solving of their problems and lessens worry about a future that is already completely predestined. Sir Isaiah Berlin, Professor of Social and Political Theory at Oxford University, observes: "Where there is no choice there is no anxiety; and a happy release from responsibility. Some human beings have always preferred the peace of imprisonment, a contented security, a sense of having at last found one's proper place in the cosmos, to the painful conflicts and perplexities of the disordered freedom of the world beyond the walls." [24] When Jawaharlal Nehru was Prime Minister of India and daily confronted with awesome responsibilities involving 400,000,000 people, he remarked to a friend that he had a feeling of "nostalgia" for his years in prison because there he had so few decisions to make.[25]

Dostoievsky depicts men's effort to elude freedom in his fable of Jesus returning to earth during the Spanish Inquisition. We see Jesus face to face with the Grand Inquisitor, who solemnly declares: ". . . nothing has ever been more insupportable for a man and a human society than freedom. . . . I tell Thee that man is tormented by no greater anxiety than to find some one quickly to whom he can hand over that gift of freedom with which the ill-fated creature is born. . . . Didst Thou forget that man prefers peace, and even death, to freedom of choice in the knowledge of good and evil?" [26] The Grand Inquisitor proposes to burn the reincarnated Jesus at the stake for his crime in placing upon man this "fearful burden of free choice." [27]

A widely read book over the past twenty years, *Escape From Freedom*, by Erich Fromm, deals with yet another aspect of the same general theme. According to the author ". . . modern man still is anxious and tempted to surrender his freedom to dictators of all kinds, or to lose it by transforming himself into a small cog in the machine, well fed, and well clothed, yet not a free man but an automaton." [28] Man's isolation in twentieth-century society is, asserts Dr. Fromm, "unbearable and the alternatives he is confronted with are either to escape from the burden of his freedom into new dependencies and submissions, or to advance to the full realization of positive freedom which is based upon the uniqueness and individuality of man." [29]

To Fromm another psychological factor in the individual's avoidance of freedom is that he does not want to be continually beset with doubts. This age-long "quest for certainty" has been a prime motivation in the working out and acceptance of religions and philosophies that offer men sure and definite answers to their most fundamental questionings. Determinism is one of the idea systems that provide such answers by promising that literally everything in the future possesses the quality of certainty by being foreordained.

Dr. Paul Kurtz, a teacher of philosophy at the State University of New York at Buffalo, declares that the main threat to individual freedom today is that men have become submerged in such organizations as business corporations, churches, government bureaus, labor unions, political parties, universities, and associations and clubs of all sorts. "Organizations," Dr. Kurtz says, "become independent entities with 'personalities' of their own. . . . One of the reasons why the individual today frequently feels powerless, impotent, and unable to affect decision-making processes in his society is that decisions emanate from organizations, not individuals; it is organizations which contend for power, not individuals. . . . The point is that individuals by themselves have been shorn of power. Moral choices are largely within the context of an organizational structure. . . . Insofar as the individual is swallowed up by the impersonal bureaucracy there is a decline in his personal responsibility and a subtle corrosion of his integrity." [30]

The freedom of choice issue has also played a major role in the fields of economics, education, history, law, psychology, psychiatry, psychoanalysis and sociology. I shall not undertake in this book to trace the implications of free choice and of determinism in all these various realms of human endeavor, but shall refer to them when it seems pertinent.

In the branch of philosophy known as ethics a persistent question is: how can we attribute ethical responsibility to men, and punish them for wrongdoing, if we accept the determinist thesis that their choices and actions are predetermined? For this means that individuals cannot help doing what they do and are therefore morally without guilt. The free choice view, however, sees men as possessing the freedom either to do or not to do what they know is right. Thus they bear full responsibility for their conduct.

Relevant to this discussion is the French dictum, "tout comprendre, c'est tout pardonner" [31] (to understand everything is to forgive everything).* This thought means that if one could know the complete chain of causation that led a criminal to an atrocious murder or a Hitler to bring war and death to millions of peace-loving people, then one would be ready to pardon the murderer or Hitler. The epigram assumes that determinism is true and that evil men are to be forgiven because they were influenced and governed by causes and reasons they were unable to resist. A

* Cf. p. 75.

liberal friend of mine from the South took the same approach when she told me that racists are not to be much blamed because, after all, they were brought up and educated to behave that way.

The freedom-determinism question frequently enters into discussions of educational technique and the degree to which parents are responsible for how their children behave. I have heard certain educators and psychiatrists talk as if parents were to blame for all the erratic, violent or anti-social tendencies of their children; and then give the children all the credit if they grow up into polite, amiable and intelligent young citizens. Or children themselves will take their father and mother to task for the way in which they were brought up.

"In recent years a new form of punishment has been imposed on middle-aged and elderly parents. Their children, now in their twenties, thirties or even forties, present them with a modern grievance: 'My analysis proves that *you* are responsible for my neurosis.' Overawed by these authoritative statements, the poor tired parents fall easy victims to the newest variations on the scapegoat theory." [32] Admittedly, no parents achieve perfection in the rearing of their children. Yet the fact is that children, too, possess freedom of choice. It appears at an early age and develops with the intelligence and other capacities of the youthful personality. Children, then, share the responsibility for their behavior and emerging characters with their parents, relatives, teachers and friends.

Thought is of critical importance in the exercise of decision at any age. It is to be remembered that the word *intelligence* originates in the Latin *inter* (between) and *legere* (to choose). However, much human activity is not the result of deliberate choice. Some of our most important functions, such as breathing and the circulation of the blood, are fortunately automatic, as long as we stay healthy. And the human embryo's development, which compresses perhaps a billion years of evolution into nine months, is a natural miracle of biological determinism.

As to conscious human actions, many of them are purely impulsive or follow from long-established habits. We often talk of others or even of ourselves as being "slaves of habit." It is an important part of man's freedom to be able to modify habits or give up harmful ones altogether. Many individuals suffer from bodily determinisms in the form of allergies, as when a man starts sneezing because a cat is in the room or because he is sensitive to certain kinds of flowers, plants or grass. Hence involuntary responses and behavior must be distinguished from the voluntary.

Every day the average person makes free choices, important or unimportant, easy or difficult in the deciding. It may be a question of what he will order for lunch, whether he will return home from work by bus or subway, what children's book he will read to his small daughter before she goes to bed. Obviously, certain choices are of particular significance for an individual, as when he decides on what life work to enter, whom to marry or where to live.

Occasionally, we find it all but impossible to choose between two or more alternatives, because we feel so unsure about which is going to work out best. Most of us have surely experienced the mental agony of indecision, sometimes lasting for a considerable period. If we then flip a coin to decide the matter, we are exercising freedom of choice by assigning responsibility for the decision to the caprice of chance. The very fact that in such a situation we decline to take direct responsibility points to the reality of free choice under ordinary circumstances.

The role of reason in freedom of choice is persuasively presented in the philosophic fable of Buridan's Ass. The ass, since he did not possess the capacity of thought, died of hunger and thirst because he was incapable of choosing between food and water that were located at two points equally distant from him. A man in a similar situation, the fable continues, would have resolved "the equilibrium of opposing motives" through deliberation and free choice. In *The Divine Comedy,* Dante discusses variations on this theme of Buridan's Ass. And Beatrice tells him: "The greatest gift which God in His bounty bestowed in creating . . . was freedom of the will, with which the creatures that have intelligence, they all and they alone, were and are endowed." [33]

On the other hand, Edgar Lee Masters in his poem "Roger Heston" in *Spoon River Anthology* suggests that animals may have free will:

Oh many times did Ernest Hyde and I
Argue about the freedom of the will.
My favorite metaphor was Prickett's cow
Roped out to grass, and free you know as far
As the length of the rope.
One day while arguing so, watching the cow

Pull at the rope to get beyond the circle
Which she had eaten bare,
Out came the stake, and tossing up her head,
She ran for us.
"What's that, free-will or what?" said Ernest, running.
I fell just as she gored me to my death.

When we explore the implications of the determinist position, we arrive at some extraordinary results. For it means that every decision and action of a man today was predestined in detail not just five months ago or five years ago, but before the human race had even come into existence. Indeed, the inexorable causal chain goes back five billion years to the whirling convulsions that marked the birth of the solar system, and into the infinite past prior to that event. By the same logic determinism implies that everything that is going to happen in the future of the cosmos, whether tomorrow or millions of years hence, is already shaped and necessitated in and by the present. Thus the whole future is somehow telescoped into the present and is fully contained in its configurations.

Professor Milič Čapek of Boston University analyzes the situation: "As the future in the deterministic framework possesses the character of absolute necessity, it acquires *ipso facto* the status of reality; it becomes something *actually* existing, a sort of disguised and hidden present which remains hidden only from our limited knowledge, just as distant regions of space are hidden from our sight. 'Future' is merely a label given by us to the unknown part of the *present* reality, which exists in the same degree as scenery hidden from our eyes. As this hidden portion of the present is *contemporary* with the portion accessible to us, the temporal relation between the present and the future is eliminated; the future loses its status of 'futurity' because instead of succeeding the present it *coexists* with it." [34]

As applied to literature, for instance, the idea of determinism connotes that every last line, phrase, word and punctuation mark in the books, plays or poetry of every writer in history were destined to emerge in the precise form they finally took.

The philosophic or religious determinist runs into additional trouble when he is compelled by force of logic to admit that his own position and the brilliant arguments supporting it are all necessitated from aeons back by the iron laws of cause and effect. And he must extend the paradox by saying that my own stand in favor of the free choice thesis is also preordained and that my faulty thinking constitutes an unfortunate inevitability in the great onrush of fate. The mind reels and revolts in the face of these extremes demanded by the determinist doctrine.

Becoming personal for a moment, I want to try to throw light on our central issue by analyzing one of my most frequent activities—public speaking. Almost always, whether at a meeting or over the radio, I speak extemporaneously from a few notes that outline the subject. As I proceed, I am continually searching for the right word, the right phrase. Sometimes I have to pause a second or two and grope for that word. I am thinking hard the whole time. And from start to finish in this process I have a constant sense of instantaneous free choices. It is impossible for me to believe that what finally issues forth in my addresses is all somehow preordained.

Speech in general is a good example of how human beings exercise freedom of choice in the ordinary course of living. However rapidly an individual talks in conversation, he is consciously choosing his words. Of course many expressions become routine, but even a simple "hello" or "goodbye" may vary in meaning according to the tone of voice in which it is spoken.

Writing brings freedom of choice into play in much the same manner as talking. I myself am a slow writer and repeatedly go back over a page, crossing out words, writing in new ones, changing the grammatical construction, inserting whole paragraphs or pages. The reader of this book would have been horrified to see what a mess it was in the first draft. In any case, the alterations I have made constitute a genuine intellectual task. It seems far-fetched to claim that this laborious process of literary trial, error and correction is all determined long in advance, and that my entire course of complex reasoning as an author is simply a masque of make-believe.

Naturally, since I am trying to produce a book on freedom of choice, it is expected that what I write herein should fit into a certain frame of reference. That frame is the self-imposed limit, freely chosen, within which my free choice as the author of this volume is supposed to operate. The control that I thereby exercise over my writing is to be described as self-discipline, not determinism.

One of the strongest supports for the free choice thesis is the unmistakable intuition of virtually every human being that he is free to make the choices he does and that his deliberations leading to those choices are also free-flowing. The normal man feels, too, after he has made a decision, that he could have decided differently.* That is why regret or remorse for a past choice can be so disturbing. One can refrain from a certain action; and that non-action is likewise a choice.

In my opinion, our inner feeling of freedom of choice is as strong as the common-sense conviction that an objective external world exists independently of our consciousness or that other human beings are part of that world. It is almost as strong as the intuitive assurance of our own existence as individuals. No doubt it was such reflections that led Dr. Johnson to inform Boswell, "We *know* our will is free, and *there's* an end on 't." [35] This introspective intuition of free choice, unlike intuitions of God, immortality, supernatural spirits and the like, is not of something beyond mortal life, but arises directly from human feeling and functioning that seem as real as pleasure or pain.

This intuition, then, which recurs day in and day out, is a datum of immediate experience. As the Utilitarian philosopher, Henry Sidgwick, says: ". . . it is unlike the erroneous intuitions which occur in the exercise of the senses; as e.g., the imperfections of sight and hearing. For experience soon teaches me to regard these as appearances whose suggestions are misleading; but no amount of experience of the sway of motives even tends to make me distrust my intui-

* Cf. pp. 152-53.

tive consciousness that in resolving after deliberation I exercise free choice as to which of the motives acting on me shall prevail." [36]

Horace M. Kallen, Professor of Social Philosophy at the New School for Social Research, asserts: "That the experience of freedom is the experience of a reality, is a belief as old as philosophy itself, and is shared no less by necessitarians who prove with argument that the belief is a disguised error than by libertarians who affirm that it is a self-evident truth. Both start from an experience of freedom, the first moving to deny, the second to confirm the reality of that *terminus a quo* [starting point]. And the deniers could not deny if they lacked the continuing freedom to search out and to devise the means whereby they strip away the disguise and expose the error." [37]

The intuitive consciousness of freedom cannot, of course, be accepted as conclusive in itself, but must be judged finally in the light of reason and of the available evidence. At the same time the intuition is so powerful that it creates an initial presumption in favor of the free choice thesis.

Some of the ablest philosophers, however, have ridiculed this intuition of freedom. One of these was Benedict Spinoza, who writes in a letter: "Conceive, I beg, that a stone, while continuing in motion, should be capable of thinking and knowing, that it is endeavoring, as far as it can, to continue to move. Such a stone, being conscious merely of its own endeavor and deeply interested therein, would believe itself to be completely free, and would think that it continued in motion solely because of its own wish.

Now such is this freedom of man's will that everyone boasts of possessing, and which consists only in this, that men are aware of their own desires and ignorant of the causes by which those desires are determined. . . . As this misconception is innate in all men, it is not easily conquered." [38]

Baron d'Holbach, one of the French Encyclopedists of the eighteenth century, employs a figure of speech similar to Spinoza's: " 'But, you will say, I feel free.' This is an illusion, that may be compared to that of the fly in the fable, who, lighting upon the pole of a heavy carriage, applauded himself for directing its course. Man, who thinks himself free, is a fly, who imagines he has power to move the universe, while he is himself unknowingly carried along by it." [39]

I must disagree with Spinoza and Holbach; and I would add that the dynamics of free choice runs so deep in human nature that even those who sincerely believe in fatalism or universal determinism *act* to a large degree as if they had freedom of choice. The Mohammedans, whose supernatural religion preaches a preordained fate for every individual, are not habitually sluggish and inactive. On the contrary, they are among the most militant warriors in history. The anti-religious Communists, whose secular philosophy promises, on the other hand, the inevitable triumph of communism everywhere through the operation of Historical Materialism and economic determinism, are among the most energetic workers for conscious goals that the world has ever seen.

To repeat the central affirmation of this book, men

possess freedom of choice and it is one of their most significant powers. This freedom, like thinking itself, is deeply grounded in human nature and is a universal characteristic of normal human beings. Since thought for the most part is instrumental to the solving of problems and since problem-solving entails selecting a correct solution, we may say that man thinks primarily in order to choose. Conversely, successful free choice requires thought. Thus man choosing is usually man thinking, and man thinking is usually man choosing.

2

Can Freedom and
Determinism Co-Exist?

When in the memorable motion picture *Lawrence of Arabia* the fatalistic Mohammedan fighters wanted to persuade Colonel Lawrence of the impossibility of one of his proposed military expeditions, they said, shaking their heads, "It is written." To which Lawrence's spirited retort was always "*Nothing* is written." The film proceeds to show how in each case he successfully urged the Arab troops on and how together they carried out the venture against tremendous odds.

Actually, Lawrence was not right, nor were the Arabs; for the truth is that in human life a great deal is inexorably determined ("written"), and a great deal derives from either chance or man's freedom of choice. Both Lawrence and the Arabs made the mistake of considering the two concepts, freedom of choice and determinism, to be mutually exclusive, as if there must be universal determinism *or* absolute freedom. Even professional philosophers have committed the same error.

To phrase our central issue as "freedom of choice *versus* determinism" would be quite misleading. For freedom and necessity do not rule each other out; they frequently go hand in hand. Indeed, throughout human existence there is an interlocking pattern of *both* in terms of *relative* determinism and *relative* freedom. The recognition of this fact is the beginning of wisdom for understanding the problem of free choice.

The first place to look for the co-existence of freedom and determinism is in the characteristic development and functioning of Homo sapiens. All normal human beings, owing to the vital determinisms working within them, will, if they remain alive, grow in bodily strength and stature to adolescence and adulthood, will develop strong sexual desires and will eventually die—though exactly when, where and how, nobody can predict. Nothing is more certain for us than death and nothing more uncertain than the precise hour at which it will strike. These deterministic predictabilities, however, which apply to man as man, do not nullify freedom of choice; they provide a framework within which it operates and thereby a focus for men's energies.

Not only man's respiratory and circulatory systems function on a deterministic basis, as I indicated earlier, but also his digestive, reproductive and ductless gland systems. These various key systems have an extraordinary capacity for self-regulation, and interact with one another and with other physiological functions to produce a complex organism with the most prodigious powers and potentialities ever evolved upon this earth. It was such considerations as these that inspired Lamettrie, a French materialist philosopher of the eighteenth century and a forerunner of the Encyclopedists, to write his book, *Man a Machine* (1748). We can accept much of what Lamettrie said about the mechanistic functioning of human beings, but he went all the way with his deterministic interpretation, and so ruled out any possibility of freedom of choice.

During the last years of the nineteenth century Ivan P. Pavlov, the Russian physiologist and psychologist, discovered the conditioned reflex through his well-known experiments with dogs. He found that the dogs, after they had repeatedly been given food when a bell was sounded, would salivate at the sound of the bell when they received no food. In man the conditioned reflex takes effect when a voluntary action is transformed into automatic reflex behavior following upon the repeated association of a particular reaction with a particular external stimulus. Thus, a beginner at driving an automobile quickly learns to stop when he sees a red light gleaming at an intersection. This stopping soon becomes a conditioned reflex rather than a genuine choice. Reflex action on the level of abstractions is also frequent, as when, after thorough training in elementary mathematics, one utilizes addition and subtraction.

The conditioned reflex or response is basic for the building of habits and constitutes an additional form of human or animal functioning with deterministic aspects.

An individual may temporarily interdict an established reflex if some unusual situation arises, as when a policeman at an intersection beckons a driver to come through a red light. The behaviorist school in psychology has made the conditioned reflex the doctrinal keystone of its mechanistic interpretation of all human choice and action. But, as I see it, conditioned reflexes can never account for the entire conscious life of a man unless all novelty disappears and every day becomes in every detail an exact replica of preceding days.

The human ability to think created an altogether new level of behavior among living creatures and led to the emergence of free choice. Thinking and choosing of course have a physical base and in their causal efficacy rely continually upon a man's internal determinants. Since animals in general are not endowed with the attribute of abstract, conceptual thought, they presumably do not have freedom of choice. Their choices are *instinctually* determined. Men have the power to *improve* on instinctual determinism through free choice and reason. They can control a powerful instinct, such as that of procreation, as when they adopt some method for planned parenthood; and they can even nullify an instinct, that of self-preservation, as when they commit suicide, or voluntarily risk or lose their lives in dedication to a cause.

The very nature of man demands and determines that when a normal person's mental capacities reach a certain stage, he will start to exercise freedom of choice. It is a deterministic law, structured in one's genetic inheritance, that free choice shall emerge. The distinguished Viennese psychiatrist, Viktor E. Frankl, develops this thought further: "If we wanted to define man, we would have to call him that entity which has freed itself from whatever has determined it (determined it as biological-psychological-sociological type): that entity, in other words, that transcends all these determinants either by conquering them and shaping them, or by deliberately submitting to them." [40]

Furthermore, every human being is a distinct individual and in his decisions functions as that individual and no other. He makes his own free choices and not those of somebody else. Nor can some other individual interpenetrate his brain and nervous system to direct his choices. The rare occurrence of hypnotism is in this context the exception that proves the rule. The natural limitation involved in each person's being his own chooser is essential to the power and significance of freedom of choice, just as the banks of a river are essential to its behaving like a river.

Coming now to *external* determinants important for man, we note that in modern times he has gained enormous control over Nature by discovering a multitude of scientific laws and then using them, according to the dictates of free choice, for his own welfare, comfort and happiness. These laws, like those that pertain to the inner functioning of man, are always the expression of if-then sequences or relations. *If* the temperature drops to 32 degrees Fahrenheit, *then* water under normal conditions freezes into ice. A strict if-then relation holds between two events only if the first invariably causes the second, and if the second cannot occur unless preceded by the first. The if-then formula well expresses the predictability that is central to the scientific enterprise.

If the temperature of water rises to 212 degrees, *then* (and here is the prediction) it will boil and a housewife will be able to produce a good meal, because if meat and vegetables are properly boiled, then (prediction again) they will make a tasty dish. One of the most useful mechanisms man has invented is the gas oven which, when lighted, makes it possible to cook a large variety of nourishing foods. In fact, the whole vast enterprise of modern cookery well illustrates the way in which human beings through freedom of choice exploit both deterministic laws discovered thousands of years ago and the new dynamic laws associated with the thousand and one mechanisms and gadgets of today's kitchen.

To take another common example, when a man wishes to go somewhere in his motorboat, he relies on its built-in determinism of self-starter, clutch, throttle and wheel. But it is he, not the boat, that decides when and where he will go. Naturally, any trip he takes is limited by his own time schedule, the amount of gasoline at his disposal and that ever-present menace—the weather. The operation of a motorboat also illustrates that in complex machines, and always in those that include the internal combustion engine, the initiation of one if-then sequence will bring into play other if-then sequences necessary for the total functioning of the machine.

In the more highly developed nations of the present the immense progress of medicine and health is primarily owing to the increased knowledge of the determinisms that function within the human body, and to the discovery of new drugs and techniques to deal with disease and disability: insulin to control diabetes, quinine to control malaria, and inoculations against smallpox, typhoid fever, polio and other diseases. All curative drugs, all measures effective against disease, are based upon if-then laws. But these laws are not self-administrating; it is physicians and surgeons, in consultation with their patients, who decide when and how to administer the drugs and medical techniques.

The science of medicine well illustrates how men are able to utilize one law or set of laws to prevent or counteract the unwanted consequences of another law or set of laws. Every serious disease acts according to its own laws when it afflicts a human being. To offset its ravages, the doctor prescribes a drug or inoculation which brings into effect a curative if-then sequence when applied to the patient's body. It usually takes a law to nullify a law.

In Professor Kallen's words: ". . . the undeterminable and utterly spontaneous are not amenable to control and to use, which are the agencies of Human Freedom. It is earthquake and tidal wave, cancer and other unconquered disease, which we cannot control, that make us afraid and keep us bond. For mankind hence the discovery of determinism is the beginning of freedom. Our knowledge of the mechanisms which work the world we live in frees us from their compulsions. To know how a thing happens is to be the master of the event, to be in a position to transform a power that commands into a power that serves." [41]

So it is that successful human living utilizes scientific

laws as *means* for the achievement of *ends* that are decided upon by individual or group freedom of choice. This process reaches its apex in a machine civilization like that of the United States today. Every machine is a man-made unit of determinism. Of course labor-saving machines and automation, through their own efficiency create new problems, especially that of unemployment.

Natural laws in general (this does not include governmental laws established by society) are ethically neutral. That is, they can be employed to promote either the good or the bad. Nature's gift of fire, with its laws, is a godsend to humanity in many ways, but can also be used to burn religious dissenters at the stake or to destroy—through explosive bombs and napalm—buildings and people in towns, cities or countryside. Nuclear power can be of enormous service to mankind, but so far has been utilized mainly as the most frightful of all weapons for armaments and war.

While human freedom expands through the wise use of natural laws, those laws at the same time limit the extent of that freedom. They set boundaries to effective action. The law of gravity is essential to the stability of houses, office buildings and skyscrapers, but it brings death to those who fall from high places. The mechanisms that enable an airplane to fly through the air prevent it from traveling under the sea like a submarine. Water helps the crops to grow, but flood will ruin both farms and farmers.

Despite these limitations, the larger the number of if-then laws an individual knows how to put into effect, the greater is his scope of action and freedom. This is the point of the adage, "Freedom is the knowledge of necessity." [42] This saying, however, in my opinion expresses a half-truth at most. For a man has maximum freedom only if he is aware of the entire situation and knows that free choice and contingency exist as well as necessity.

There are several qualifications to the functioning of deterministic if-then laws. In the first place, an event utterly irrelevant to a specific law may, and sometimes does, intrude between the occurrence of the *if* factor and the *then* factor that would ordinarily follow. One evening I turned on the switch as usual to light the electric lamp in my living room, and nothing happened. Then I discovered that the lights throughout the house were out and that a gray squirrel had caused a short-circuit (and electrocuted himself) by climbing a Consolidated Edison pole and biting into the main wire carrying electric power into my house. Again, on a bitterly cold morning I manipulated my car's self-starter to get the engine going, but the battery would not work because of the zero weather.

To summarize this matter in general terms: "In any one determinate system such as mechanics or economics, the proposition 'the event B will occur' may be the inevitable logical consequence of the proposition 'the event A will occur.' But in the physical world nothing is inevitable, for some event C which is not a member of that particular system may occur and prevent the occurrence of B." [43]

In the second place, science in general has more and more given up the aim of achieving *absolute* truth in factual inquiry and has been expressing scientific findings, predictions and laws in terms of various degrees of probability.

This reliance on probabilism extends to the if-then patterns already described as the domain of determinism.*

In the third place, modern science regards the very principle of causality as a fundamental *postulate* that is necessary to the whole scientific enterprise. Postulates are general assumptions that are presupposed in all scientific factual inquiry, but which can never be absolutely proved. The postulate of causality assumes that the cause-effect relation has applied, does apply and will apply to all events in the cosmos. Tied in closely with this postulate is that of the uniformity of Nature or predictive uniformity, which assumes that in our world "a given group of events will show in subsequent experience the same kind and degree of interconnection that they have shown already." [44]

The two basic postulates described have been demonstrated as sound in an enormous number of cases and indeed throughout the entire history of science, but we cannot be 100 per cent sure that they will hold for all future time during its untold decillions of years. Meanwhile, these postulates remain regulative and guiding principles that continue to prove justified in every new scientific discovery and in the everyday life of mankind.

There is another form of necessity in addition to that exemplified by fixed uniformities in Nature. That is the necessity involved in deduction, as illustrated in the traditional Aristotelian system of logic or in the Euclidean system of mathematics. The deductive method has been of

* Cf. p. 94.

immense importance in the advance of the various sciences. The laws of the syllogism demand that if a certain major premise and a certain minor premise are given, then a certain conclusion is bound to follow. To cite the classic example: All men are mortal; Socrates is a man; therefore Socrates is mortal. In correct deduction one statement follows from another *necessarily* if it follows at all; but of course no causation is involved. These same principles hold for mathematics. For instance, it is *logically* inevitable for an odd number always immediately to succeed an even number.

To think, however, that in the world of concrete reality, causes and effects stand in the same relation as do premises and their conclusions in logic, is to confuse the temporal meaning of "follows" with its logical, non-temporal meaning.* As Professor Čapek explains in his penetrating article, "The Doctrine of Necessity Re-Examined": "Only when causal connection is *not* conceived as a deductive implication, can it retain its dynamic successive character which appears as a foreign and unaccountable element in the necessitarian scheme." [45]

Professor Charles Hartshorne of the University of Texas pursues the argument and suggests that historically speaking the determinist fallacy originated mainly from a misunderstanding of the relation between deductive and inductive reasoning: "Deduction gives certainty, necessity, exactitude; induction gives probability, more or less irresistible tendencies, approximations. Since the certain and

* See John Dewey, "The Superstition of Necessity," *The Monist* (April, 1893), pp. 362-79.

absolute knowledge derived from mathematics is flattering to our sense of power, it is natural that we should try to interpret our scientific discoveries in accordance with the mathematical ideal, especially since mathematics, being the simplest science, was the first to achieve a high technical development (Euclidean geometry). . . . It is a fact that modern determinism arose in an age which did not adequately appreciate the inductive character of scientific method, the age of Descartes and Spinoza; and that the ancient determinists were the Stoics, the champions of deduction, whereas the Epicureans, who believed in chance and freedom, were the apostles of induction." [46]

The truth is that many thinkers in the West have read the deductive determinism relevant only to sound reasoning into the behavior of all objects and events in the great cosmic kaleidoscope. So impressed were they by the triumphs of science during the past 500 years in discovering and establishing reliable if-then patterns that they came to believe that *everything* on earth and in the universe is governed by natural law. These are major reasons for the considerable prestige of determinism during the nineteenth and twentieth centuries, and for the fact that it is supported by some of the most brilliant philosophers and scientists of the present era. To many individuals determinism has been almost like an article of religious faith.

Says Professor Sidney Hook of New York University: "During the twentieth century the overwhelming majority of historians have been in unconscious thralldom to one or another variety of social determinism." [47] As for American psychology, its predominant attitude, according to Professor Carl A. Rogers, Fellow of the Western Behavioral Sciences Institute, is to treat man as a mere object to be scientifically controlled and to deny the existence of personal freedom or free choice. In a 1964 paper, "Freedom and Commitment," Professor Rogers asserts: "In the minds of most behavioral scientists, man is not free, nor can he as a free man commit himself to some purpose, since he is controlled by factors outside of himself. Therefore, neither freedom nor commitment is even a possible concept in modern behavioral science as it is usually understood." [48]

Speaking of modern "philosophies of exculpation," Joseph Wood Krutch, one of America's most perceptive writers, tells us: "Since dogmas do not have to be accepted in their full dogmatic rigidity in order to have a very powerful effect, the question of how clearly and how absolutely deterministic theories are held is of relatively little importance. What is important is the evident fact that educational, sociological and even criminological principles and methods have come increasingly to focus attention and effort on that aspect of man and his behavior which seems most easily interpreted in accordance with such theories, so that even when man is not openly proclaimed to be no more than a 'product' of 'conditions' he is treated as though he were." [49]

Albert Einstein, one of the great physicists of all time, was much influenced by Spinoza and was a philosophic determinist. Einstein writes: "The more a man is imbued with the ordered regularity of *all* events, the firmer becomes his conviction that there is no room left side by side of this ordered regularity for causes of a different nature. . . ." [50] "Without the belief that it is possible to grasp the reality with our theoretical constructions, without the belief in *the inner harmony* of our world, there could be no science." [51] [Italics mine—C. L.]

Hazardous as it is to disagree with so profound a thinker as Einstein, I am compelled to say that the above statements are erroneous. It is a serious fallacy to consider causality synonymous with "the ordered regularity of all events." That regularity or uniformity does *not* apply to all events and their causes, but only to a certain class of them. For side by side with the immutable laws that constitute cosmic necessity there is the broad realm of contingency or chance. The existence of chance negates the possibility of complete "harmony" in the universe. Science, however, can and does proceed successfully by discovering more and more if-then relations that represent regularity and harmony in the world.

3

Contingency and
a Pluralistic World

If absolute determinism rules throughout the universe, including our earth, then the great cosmic Juggernaut inexorably rolls on; and all human thoughts, choices and actions were totally predetermined billions of years ago. Then, indeed, that "ordered regularity of all events," of which Einstein speaks, becomes a fundamental truth, and everything that exists necessarily falls into the pattern of if-then laws. Democritus, Marcus Aurelius, Spinoza, Hegel and Bertrand Russell are some of the eminent philosophers who have upheld this viewpoint.

Other thinkers in the history of philosophy deny the determinist thesis and find that one of the ultimate, irreducible traits of the cosmos is chance, contingency, indeterminism or fortuity.* Outstanding philosophers such as

* Another and rather esoteric synonym for contingency is *tychism*, which stems from the Greek *tyche*, meaning *chance*. In the ancient Greek polytheistic religion, one of the most popular

Aristotle, Epicurus, William James, Henri Bergson and John Dewey insist that what we call *chance* is not merely a word for expressing subjective human ignorance of cause and effect, but that chance exists objectively outside of and regardless of the human mind. In fact, chance may well have been responsible not only for the birth of our solar system, but for many of those mutations in biological evolution which culminated in the appearance of Homo sapiens upon this planet.

When I refer to chance or contingency as an ultimate trait of the universe, I mean that it is one of those basic categories of *existence as such* that constitute one's metaphysics or ontology. Such categories denote the least common denominators of everything that exists. In Aristotle's words, metaphysics is the science ". . . which investigates being as being and the attributes which belong to this in virtue of its own nature. Now this is not the same as any of the so-called special sciences; for none of these others treats universally of being as being. They cut off a part of being and investigate the attributes of this part. . . . All these sciences mark off some particular being—some genus, and inquire into this, but not into being simply nor *qua* being." [52]

The term *star* is important in astronomy, but there are no stars in biology; the term *animal* is important in biology, but does not help to explain the behavior of stars. However, the terms *substance, activity, relation* and *causality* are all fundamental in astronomy, biology and every other science. They are true metaphysical categories. There can be no

---

deities was Tyche, the Goddess of Chance or Fortune. The counterpart Roman divinity was Fors Fortuna.

explanation of *why* these particular generic traits exist; they simply *are*. To demand a reason for their existence is as futile as asking the cause of causality.

In science as well as philosophy it has frequently become fruitless to keep on asking, "Why?" At such a juncture the scientist can only say, "Things are simply constructed this way or behave that way." Einstein regarded the speed of light, the fastest thing in the universe, as an absolute and did not try to find out *why* it travels at the rate of approximately 186,300 miles per second. Physicists cannot give an intelligible answer as to why there is only one electron whirling around the nucleus in a hydrogen atom and ninety-two electrons revolving in the uranium atom.* Clearly, then, we eventually hit rock bottom in scientific investigations; and the same holds true for philosophic inquiries, especially those dealing with the ultimates of existence.

Contingency as a cosmic ultimate has necessity or determinism as its correlative. These two metaphysical traits are complementary counterparts that imply each other and involve a reciprocal relationship like that of *north* and *south*, *odd* and *even*, *hot* and *cold*. Contingency and necessity are *both* pervasive and permanent attributes of the universe, and neither can ever swallow up the other, any more than substance or activity can force each other out of existence.

* Cf. the statement by Dean E. Woolridge, Research Associate at the California Institute of Technology: "The scientist delineates the orderly and predictable interactions among the quantities; he never explains the quantities themselves." (*New York Times Magazine,* Oct. 4, 1964.)

In the narrower sense the quality of being contingent means that one event is dependent on the occurrence of another event, as when we say that international peace is contingent on mutual understanding among the countries concerned. However, the more fundamental meaning of the contingent and contingency is much wider. A broad philosophic definition of contingency or chance is that it is simply the opposite of determinism or necessity, meaning that an event, object or state of affairs either may or may not be. This does *not* imply that any event is causeless.

In his definitive book on Aristotle, Professor John H. Randall, Jr., of Columbia University sharpens our definition: "The distinction between what occurs by chance and what does not is not a distinction between what has a cause and what has no cause; it is rather a distinction between two kinds of events, all of which have determinate causes. To occur 'by chance' means, not that there is no reason for the accident, but that factors, themselves determined by their own specific causes, do impinge on other processes, and alter and perhaps even destroy them, without being an essential part of those other processes, without belonging to their distinctive nature. . . .*

"For instance, a rock falls on the acorn and distorts its growth, or a squirrel eats it, and it never sprouts. These events have no relevance to the process of growing into an

---

* Cf. the late H. W. B. Joseph, my tutor in philosophy at New College, Oxford: "Few people really believe that anything happens without a cause; but chance is not the negation of cause; it is the coincidence of attributes in one individual, or events in the same moment, when each has its cause, but not the same cause, and neither helps to account for the other." (*An Introduction to Logic*, p. 78.)

oak tree, they are 'chance' events, an instance of a process 'by violence' . . . from the outside. Chance is the name given to all events caused by factors that are not relevant to the ends of natural processes, by all the non-teleological factors, the brute events interfering with the natural working out of a process, or achieving a quite different end incidentally, causing the acorn to become a squirrel's breakfast, impinging in the process 'by violence' from without." [53]

Professor Randall sums up the meaning of chance as residing in "the causal intersections of unrelated causal series." [54] I am stressing this useful definition of contingency as the conjunction of two or more events which have not been bound together in any sort of regular if-then sequence. Such conjunctions are continually occurring between mutually independent *event-series* that may be totally determined within themselves, but whose crossing at a certain location in space-time is not involved in, or predictable from, the laws or causal connections that may be operative within each series. Multiple, independent lines of causation, infinite in number, exist throughout Nature.

The characteristic operation of scientific law, far from ruling out contingency, actually implies it. For in any if-then relation, the law itself does not bring about the occurrence of the particular *if* factor; nor does Nature guarantee or command that it take place. The very meaning of *if* as a conditional conjunction requires that the *if* factor be contingent; a law does not and cannot take effect unless an event outside of its scope, and contingent in relation to it, triggers it into operation. Contingency is continually initiating necessity.

Professor Sterling P. Lamprecht explains our point in his illuminating study, *Nature and History:* "We say, and we are entitled to say, 'If this is done, then such-and-such will ensue.' But the *if* of this statement is as metaphysically evident as the *then.* The *if* is as truly a recognition of the contingency of the efficient factor of which the law does not even try to give an account, as the *then* is a recognition of the necessity of the outcome. . . . Necessity and contingency, so far from being unconnected ideas to be taken, one wholesale and the other retail, are supplementary ideas which belong together in the analysis of every separate event." [55]

In his essay, "Man's Place in Nature," Professor Lamprecht provides further light: "Contingency is often regarded as an alternative to mechanism. In fact it is a correlative aspect of nature's ways. In our world we find that forces, once initiated, work out to their inevitable consequences. But the initiation of forces is not itself decreed. The laws of nature are statements of the mechanical phase of nature. They state the uniformities of correlation and sequence that events manifest. The laws of nature are not, however, dictates that compel procedure—they are not statutes or prescriptive enactments. The presence of contingency in nature is not evident at a glance because it is not effectively exploited by inanimate agents. Inanimate agents react to the actual stimulus of the moment; they react, it might be said, to the superficial. Intelligent agents react to more than the actual stimulus; they react to the potentialities of the actual. And these potentialities are always plural. . . . The alternative possibilities were present in nature from the start even though they received no notable exploitation until intelligent creatures came to pass." [56]

I trust it is clear by this time that the existence of chance or contingency demolishes the case for a completely determined universe, and thus makes possible freedom of choice, without guaranteeing its actualization. Contingency was a reality in the cosmos during millions and billions of years before the race of man evolved; yet there was no free choice, because there were no intelligent beings who could take advantage of the openings presented by contingency. These openings come in the unending surge of alternate or plural potentialities.

I hold that human life, like Nature in the large, is shot through with contingency. When chance manifests itself in human affairs, it is frequently described as accident, coincidence or luck—good luck or bad luck. The 150 or more individuals who are struck dead by lightning every year in the United States are victims of chance in the form of extremely bad luck. On the other hand, a friend of mine encountered objective chance in the form of very good luck when, having missed his airplane flight by five minutes because his taxi was held up in a bad traffic jam, he also missed death when the jet in question crashed and burned. Most of us are acquainted with individuals who seem to be blessed with unusual luck, persons who get "all the breaks."

Chance events of one kind or another are a frequent occurrence in the life of the average man. We often go to considerable pains to guard against the possible bad results of chance happenings, as when we put up lightning rods on top of a frame house to prevent fire from lightning, or take out fire insurance. Many of the events that have been considered religious miracles were undoubtedly instances of chance.

The most readily recognized examples of chance or contingency are dramatic accidents in which independently initiated causal series or event-streams meet. I have classified death from lightning as a chance event because we can find no common, relevant cause that brings a man and a stroke of lightning into conjunction at precisely 4:15 P.M. on the eighth hole of the town golf links or at a certain turn in the street when the victim is walking home from work. We can say that in either case the individual concerned was foolish not to take shelter indoors when the thunderstorm broke, but that does not alter the role of contingency in the situation.

I have remembered for more than fifty years how one afternoon when I was about twelve years old I ran for home through a thunderstorm that was unloosing rain in sheets and torrents. I was within 100 yards of our house and dashing past a big oak when a dazzling fork of lightning blasted the tree on the side nearest me. I figured that I escaped death by about three feet. Next day I went out to look at the tree and found that the lightning had torn off a long strip of bark where it struck. It was sheer luck that I was not hit.

Actually, the lightning's striking the tree was a case of objective chance wholly within the non-human world. There were hundreds of other tall trees in the neighborhood that the lightning might have hit. This contingency situation is seen even more clearly when lightning strikes a tree in a thickly forested area where there are *millions* of other similar trees. Biochemists have recently been discussing the possibility that it was chance strokes of lightning that triggered the phenomenon of life into existence. The hypothesis is that lightning, acting upon certain kinds of inanimate matter, created the amino acids that are the building blocks of the proteins that are the primary substances in all living forms.

Consider now the unfortunate fate of an unsuspecting citizen of New York City as reported in the New York *Herald Tribune* of May 28, 1944: "A ten-pound slab of ornamental stone fell from the sixteenth floor of the Hotel Ansonia, Broadway and Seventy-third Street, at 4 P.M. yesterday and struck Miss Helen Beebe, hotel telephone operator, on the head, killing her instantly. . . . Miss Beebe had just quit her post at the hotel's telephone exchange and was walking south on the west side of Broadway when the stone struck her." *

That accident was very bad luck for Miss Beebe and a very good example of objective chance. For it represented the sudden conjunction of two presumably independent event-sequences: Miss Beebe as a human being and the loosened stone slab falling off near the top of the hotel. Naturally, if a rejected and aggrieved suitor had pushed the stone loose to take revenge on Miss Beebe, her death would not have been a case of contingency.

Let us look at an even more disastrous instance of contingency. I refer to the collision in mid-air over Chesapeake

* Since I sometimes took lunch at the Ansonia during the World War II years, I had a personal interest in Miss Beebe's accident. The stone slab might have hit me.

Bay on November 23, 1962, between a United Airlines Viscount and two whistling swans weighing some eight pounds each. When the bodies of the birds penetrated the tail mechanism of the plane, the pilot lost control and the Viscount plummeted to the ground. All seventeen persons aboard were killed. This was the first airplane accident involving whistling swans in the record of the Federal Aviation Agency.*

My favorite example of contingency is the catastrophe that took place, on April 14, 1912, when in the middle of a clear, calm night the White Star liner *Titanic,* running at full speed, hit a huge iceberg in the North Atlantic. Approximately two-thirds of the passengers and crew met their death after the ship went down about three hours following the crash. The available lifeboats could carry only 1,178 persons, whereas 2,207 were on board. From the nature of the case we can be sure that there was no conjoint initiating cause acting simultaneously on the *Titanic,* sailing from Southampton on April 10, and upon the iceberg, drifting inexorably south, that impelled them to their ocean rendezvous southeast of Newfoundland. It was obviously a chance happening.

Yet even if a team of scientific experts had been able, *per impossible,* to trace back the two causal streams and ascertain that the collision had been predestined from the very moment when the *Titanic* departed from England, that

* Cf. a news dispatch from Pakistan in *The New York Times* of Feb. 3, 1966: "Twenty-three persons were killed today when a vulture flew into the blades of a helicopter and the craft crashed, in flames. . . . An eyewitness said the vulture hit the helicopter's rotor blades, snapping one off."

conclusion would not upset my thesis. For the space-time relation of the iceberg and the *Titanic*, as the ship started on its voyage, was itself a matter of contingency, since there was no relevant cause to account for that precise relationship.

It is essential to understand that chance or contingency does not *do* anything; it is the name we give a particular type of occurrence. Nor does contingency abolish causation; on the contrary, it points to a special kind of causation, a cause-effect sequence that is happening for the first time and is therefore unique. There was no law compelling the *Titanic* and the iceberg to meet; there could have been such a law only if numerous collisions between the *Titanic* and the iceberg had occurred, all under identical conditions. But there was only one such collision, and it sent the *Titanic* to the bottom of the sea.

Applying Professor Randall's definition of chance, we see that tangling with an iceberg was not part of the *Titanic*'s "distinctive nature"; and that the wandering iceberg was manifestly one of those "factors, themselves determined by their own specific causes" that "impinge on other processes, and alter and perhaps even destroy them, without being an essential part of those other processes." *

It is to be noted, too, that once the *Titanic* had run into the iceberg, all sorts of natural laws (necessity) came into operation. That is why the impact opened up a big hole in the steamer, why the ocean water then rushed in, why the ship filled and sank, and why some 1,500 persons thrown

* See p. 59.

into the icy sea—28 degrees—soon perished from drowning or exhaustion. Of course chance, too, re-entered the scene after the *Titanic* foundered. This was particularly true for the thirty passengers and members of the crew who jumped off the ship as it went down and luckily found themselves near the overturned, but floating, collapsible surf-boat B. One by one they clambered onto her and were rescued hours later by the *S. S. Carpathia,* which picked up all survivors in the *Titanic's* lifeboats.

Naturally, the determinists dissent from my interpretation of the *Titanic's* encounter with the iceberg. Professor Gardner Williams of the University of Toledo comments: "It seems very obvious to me that the meeting was jointly caused by the natural forces in the two series. It was 100 per cent predetermined. It was an accident only because nobody foresaw or intended it. The 1,500 passengers' beliefs that they would reach New York were false from the start." [57]

Thomas Hardy takes the determinist view in his poem, "The Convergence of the Twain: Lines on the Loss of the Titanic." He finds that "The immanent Will that stirs and urges everything"

> Prepared a sinister mate
> For her—so gaily great—
> A Shape of Ice, for the time far and dissociate.
>
> And as the smart ship grew
> In stature, grace and hue,
> In shadowy silent distance grew the Iceberg too.

Alien they seemed to be:
No mortal eye could see
The intimate welding of their later history.

Or sign that they were bent
By paths coincident
On being anon twin halves of one august event.

Till the Spinner of the Years
Said "Now!" And each one hears,
And consummation comes, and jars two hemispheres.[58]

In another convincing illustration of contingency I myself was one of the chief factors. About 5:30 P.M. on Saturday, July 20, 1963, at Tamworth, New Hampshire, I was trying to view the total eclipse of the sun by the moon due to take place that afternoon. Through dark glasses I could see that the sun was being blotted out, when suddenly a white cloud drifted into my field of vision and temporarily spoiled the spectacle. Now in this case there were *three* coordinates: the eclipse, the cloud and myself. How could a determinist sensibly maintain that some common cause in ages past had brought the eclipse, the cloud and me all into our respective positions on that July afternoon, so that my view of the eclipse was obscured for five or ten minutes? Was it not clearly a chance concatenation of events?

So far I have given examples of contingency centering around interactions between human beings and inanimate objects or forces. But interactions between human individuals demonstrate objective chance just as well. For instance, in October of 1964 an unemployed Frenchwoman, Miss

Denise Rey-Herme, apparently bent on suicide, jumped off the north tower of Notre Dame Cathedral in Paris. Landing 225 feet below, she struck an American tourist, Miss Veronica McConnell. Both women were killed instantly.[59] Miss McConnell had stopped to take some photographs and had just turned to rejoin her tour group. Indisputably, there was no interacting relevant cause to account for the French lady's jumping at the exact moment she did and Miss Mc-Connell's being at the precise spot where the body fell. The accident was really an accident and not predetermined.

All of us experience contingency at first hand in our relations with other people. Perhaps the most common mode is a totally unforeseen meeting with a friend or relative. On the morning of August 9, 1965, my wife and I were leaving fascinating Mont St. Michel when we unexpectedly met, as we were approaching our car to drive away, three American friends who were just arriving. Thirty seconds more and we would have missed them altogether. We had not seen them for several years and had no idea they were anywhere in France. We all walked over to a little restaurant, drank coffee and chatted for half an hour or so. The fact that my wife and I, on the one hand, and our friends, on the other, both had a general interest in the historic and aesthetic aspects of Mont St. Michel was not a sufficiently pinpointing cause to account for our meeting at approximately ten o'clock on that particular day. The encounter obviously represented a chance intersection of two mutually independent event-streams.

Chance plays a dominant role in automobile collisions, which in the United States alone account for more than

20,000 deaths every year. However, not all such accidents are a matter of contingency. Professor Randall discusses the matter: "A car proceeds down a road at a hundred miles an hour, and collides with another. This is not chance, but an instance of a regular causal relation between speed and disaster. But if I am driving sedately and am struck by the speeding car, that is a case of chance. To be sure, *if* I had seen the other car in time, I could have avoided the collision. That is freedom, dependent on an if-then sequence, on a hypothetically necessary regular causal relation." [60] In other words, an individual is able to put into effect an if-then law to avert the impingement of a chance event that can be expected to precipitate another if-then sequence that will have disastrous consequences.

To return to the sinking of the *Titanic*, had Captain Smith heeded several wireless warnings about icebergs and cut down the speed of the ship, or had radar been in operation at the time, the disaster in all probability would not have taken place.* Even if it had not occurred, however, objective chance would still have been present. For the oncoming *Titanic* would have had to alter its course in order to avoid the impending collision; and at that point the positions of the steamer and the iceberg in relation to each other would still have been a matter of contingency.

Intercrossings of initially unrelated causal series, examples of which I have been giving, are unpredictable, but are to a large extent causally explicable *after* the event.

---

* Cf. Professor F. J. E. Woodbridge's oft-repeated story of the locomotive engineer who remarked: "In my time I have foreseen and avoided many inevitable accidents."

For contingent happenings, like all others, take place in the present; as soon as they have occurred, they become a part of history. And history can always be analyzed in terms of cause and effect.

Official investigations of the *Titanic* tragedy in both America and England showed that the steamer was running full speed in the middle of the night because the Captain had received sealed orders from the owners to try to make a record crossing of the Atlantic; and that the ship's officers were negligent in not becoming alerted by the rapid drop in the temperature, due to many icebergs being in the vicinity, during the afternoon and early evening preceding the collision.[61] As for icebergs in the North Atlantic, it was later learned that they generally form in Baffin Bay off the west coast of Greenland and drift south at the rate of one-half knot an hour. These various findings throw a good deal of light on why the *Titanic* collided with an iceberg, but do not provide an ultimate explanation of why chance befell in just that way. In truth, no such explanation was or is possible.

In the case of the young Frenchwoman leaping from the top of Notre Dame and killing a U.S. tourist below, her lack of employment was undoubtedly a major reason for her committing suicide. And Miss McConnell, the unlucky American who was hit by the falling body, had delayed a few minutes because, as an amateur photographer, she wanted to take her own pictures of the ancient Cathedral. Such facts help to explain the occurrence of the two deaths, but they do not and cannot account for the irreducible contingency that was an essential element in the tragedy.

Past events, whether embodying contingency or not, are irreversible and irrevocable. The fact that each past happening had a cause gives rise to the illusion that each was absolutely necessary and determined. But that illusion is overcome as soon as one understands that the existence of chance as a cosmic ultimate means that there are *contingent* causes, as well as causes bound up with necessity.

For centuries scholars have argued back and forth concerning the role of accident or contingency in the history of mankind. To me it seems self-evident that chance has played an important part in historical events. For instance, in February 1933 an anarchist by the name of Joseph Zangara tried to murder President-elect Franklin D. Roosevelt in Miami, Florida, as he was riding in an automobile with Mayor Cermak of Chicago. An agile woman, who happened to be standing next to the assassin, seized his arm as he was about to shoot, and the bullet intended for Roosevelt hit Cermak, who soon died from the wound.

Had Roosevelt been killed, John Nance Garner, a fourth-rate Texas politician, would have become President for at least four years, and the American Government's policies, both domestic and foreign, would probably have been of a very different character. Since the weight of the United States is so great in international affairs, Garner's accession to the Presidency would have had a considerable effect on other countries. In short, chance as exemplified in the split-second deflection of a bullet by the quick action of an alert

American had most significant consequences for both the United States and the world at large.

"The American Revolution might have ended in its infancy if there had not been a thick fog on the night when Washington withdrew his defeated army from Long Island to Manhattan. Rainy, mud-producing weather helped the French to defeat the Prussians at the Battle of Valmy and thus to save the French Revolution. . . . The turning point in the history of this country may well have been Lee's loss of the Battle of Gettysburg; Lee said later—and many agree with him—that he would have won if Stonewall Jackson had been present; but a few months earlier, Jackson had been accidentally shot by his own soldiers." [62]

At the conclusion of the American Revolutionary War, numerically superior American and French troops were besieging General Cornwallis at Yorktown. Cornwallis decided to try to escape from the trap by moving his army by night across the York River and did in fact succeed in so transporting some of his soldiers. However, a severe storm arose and prevented him from going through with the operation. Only a few days later, on October 19, 1781, Cornwallis was forced to surrender and the war was virtually terminated.

Oscar Handlin, Professor of History at Harvard University, comments on these decisive events: "The atmospheric conditions that brought on the storm and the military conditions that caused Cornwallis's army to retreat were the product of altogether separate chains of causes and effects." [63] In short, the causal sequence eventuating in stormy weather and the causal sequence represented by the military disposition of the Franco-American and British forces, no element in either sequence having been causally connected with any element in the other, met in the midst of things to form a typical chance happening. This chance happening led directly to the final defeat of Cornwallis at that particular time.[64]

History shows, too, how small contingencies in their consequences can loom large in the destiny of men and of nations. A well-known maxim of Benjamin Franklin in *Poor Richard's Almanac* reads: "A little neglect may breed mischief; for want of a nail the shoe was lost; for want of a shoe the horse was lost; for want of a horse the rider was lost." And, we may add, for want of a rider the kingdom or the battle or the cease-fire was lost. Utilizing an analogy from non-human Nature, Émile Boutroux, a French philosopher, observed that a grain dropped by a bird could start a landslide.

The volume of fascinating essays entitled *If; or, History Rewritten*[65] speculates about a number of the great might-have-been's of the past. In this book writers ranging from Warden H. A. L. Fisher of New College, Oxford, to G. K. Chesterton and Winston Churchill deploy their imaginative gifts to envision what could or might have happened at certain critical junctures in history that involved famous personages. However far-fetched some of the essays in the collection may be, they all point to the truth that human history is not a matter of rigid determinism, but is continually affected by the criss-crossings of contingency and by the free flow of individual choices, whether they be made by commanders of armies, heads of state or the common man.

Outstanding among recent books on the subject of determinism and freedom in history is *Historical Inevitability* by Sir Isaiah Berlin. Sir Isaiah vigorously attacks the idea of an all-inclusive determinism in the historical process. He sets the theme of his book in the opening paragraph where he cites sympathetically Bernhard Berenson's disenchantment with "the doctrine, lapped up in my youth, about the inevitability of events and the Moloch still devouring us today, 'historical inevitability.' I believe less and less in these more than doubtful and certainly dangerous dogmas, which tend to make us accept whatever happens as irresistible and foolhardy to oppose." [66]

Commenting on this statement, Sir Isaiah writes: "The great critic's words are particularly timely at a moment when there is, at any rate among philosophers of history, if not among historians, a tendency to return to the ancient view that all that is, is ('objectively viewed') best; that to explain is ('in the last resort') to justify; or that to know all is to forgive all; ringing falsehoods (charitably described as half-truths) which have led to special pleading and, indeed, obfuscation of the issue on a heroic scale." [67]

In a provocative passage Sir Isaiah outlines what we must come to if the inevitability doctrine is true: "To blame and praise, consider possible alternative courses of action, damn or congratulate historical figures for acting as they do or did, becomes an absurd activity. Admiration and contempt for this or that individual may indeed continue, but it becomes akin to aesthetic judgment. We can eulogize or denounce, feel love or hatred, satisfaction and shame, but we can neither blame nor alter. Alexander, Caesar, Attila, Mohammed, Cromwell, Hitler are like floods and earthquakes, sunsets, oceans, mountains; we may admire or fear them, welcome or curse them, but to denounce or extol their acts is as sensible as addressing sermons to a tree (as Frederick the Great pointed out with his customary pungency in the course of his attack on d'Holbach's deterministic *System of Nature*)." [68]

Sir Isaiah finds that the deterministic interpretation of history is frequently incorporated in some vast, vague, impersonal abstraction such as the Collective Unconscious, the German Spirit, the Master Race, Manifest Destiny, Faustian man, the Proletariat, the Life-Force, the Zeitgeist (Spirit of the Age) and History itself. Large causal entities of this sort, serving much the same function as an omni-causal and supernatural God, are regarded as the Powers-that-be in human existence, and men as mere marionettes who do their bidding.

Historical Inevitability argues that determinism logically pursued turns all history into a moral judgment. This accords with Hegel's aphorism, adapted from Frederick Schiller, that "World history is the world court." Without actually claiming that freedom of choice exists, Sir Isaiah holds that a truly deterministic world would eliminate all sense of individual responsibility. He sees the belief in determinism as "one of the great *alibis*, pleaded by those who cannot and do not wish to face the facts of human responsibility, the existence of a limited but nevertheless real area of human freedom. . . ." [69] As an example of the alibi function of determinism, Sir Isaiah recalls that Mussolini, when he learned in 1943 that the Anglo-American forces had landed in Sicily, is reported to have exclaimed, "History has seized us by the throat." The meaning of this remark was, according to Sir Isaiah, that "Men could be fought; but once 'History' herself took the field, resistance was vain." [70]

Historical Inevitability touched off a brisk debate in England. Professor Edward H. Carr, a Fellow of Trinity College, Cambridge, came forward in his book *What Is History?* to defend the inevitability interpretation and to denounce the notion that contingency intrudes. Professor Carr writes: "How can one discover in history a coherent sequence of cause and effect, how can we find any meaning in history, when our sequence is liable to be broken or deflected at any moment by some other, and from our point of view irrelevant sequence? . . . Everything that the devotees of chance and contingency in history say is perfectly true and perfectly logical. It has the kind of remorseless logic which we find in *Alice in Wonderland* and *Through the Looking Glass*." [71]

Carr criticizes Sir Isaiah for insisting that it is the duty of the historian "to judge Charlemagne or Napoleon or Genghis Khan or Hitler or Stalin for their massacres." This view, Carr replies, was "sufficiently castigated" by Professor Knowles of Cambridge University, who cited two instances of moral judgments on individuals "not within the competence of the historian to pronounce." These were

Motley's* denunciation of Philip II, "if there are vices
. . . from which he was exempt, it is because it is not per-
mitted by human nature to attain perfection even in evil,"
and Stubbs's characterization of King John, "polluted with
every crime that could disgrace a man." Knowles's verdict,
quoted by Carr, is: "The historian is not a judge, still less a
hanging judge." [72]

However, Carr does concede that even when Sir Isaiah
"talks nonsense, he earns our indulgence by talking it in an
engaging and attractive way. The disciples repeat the nonsense, and fail to make it attractive." [73] Then, commenting
on the idea that no "inevitable sequence" can exist in history, Carr makes a rapier thrust: "It is Professor Popper**
and Sir Isaiah Berlin who between them have flogged this
very dead horse back into a semblance of life; and some
patience will be required to clear up the muddle." [74]

The controversy spilt over into the pages of the *Lis-
tener*, weekly publication of the British Broadcasting Cor-
poration, in which Carr and Sir Isaiah exchanged hard-
hitting letters. The latter's rebuttal says in part, "we cannot
really embrace determinism, that is, incorporate it in our
thought and action, without far more revolutionary changes
in our language and outlook (some among them scarcely
imaginable in terms of our ordinary words and ideas) than
are dreamt of in Mr. Carr's philosophy." [75]

Probably the most fiercely disputed form of historic
determinism during the past 100 years or more has been

* John Lothrop Motley, American historian of the nineteenth
century.
** Karl R. Popper, author of *The Open Society and Its Enemies*.

the *economic* determinism propounded by Marxists and Communists the world over. Karl Marx and Frederick Engels applied their theory of the economic interpretation of history not only to politics, but to the whole of social and cultural life. According to their doctrine of Historical Materialism, the underlying factor in the course of history is not merely the natural conditions of production, such as the supply of raw materials and the characteristics of geography, nor merely the techniques of production, such as the state of metallurgy and of machine processes. What is determining is the *total relations* of production and exchange, the entire economic structure of society.

These total economic relations express themselves at any given time in certain *property* relations which are crystallized in definite class forms covering all aspects of civilized life. This is why for Marx and Engels class struggles, often masked in religious or nationalist movements or wars, have played the central role in human affairs. The class struggle reaches a climax in the opposition between the capitalist class and the working class, with the latter eventually attaining power *inevitably* in every nation and constructing the new classless society of communism.

In *The Communist Manifesto* of 1848 Marx and Engels proclaim: "What the bourgeoisie therefore produces, above all, are its own grave-diggers. Its downfall and the victory of the proletariat are equally inevitable." [76] In his Preface to the first edition of *Capital* (1867) Marx writes: "Intrinsically, it is not a question of the higher or lower degree of development of the social antagonisms that result from the natural laws of capitalist production. It is a question of these laws themselves, of *these tendencies working with iron necessity towards inevitable results.*" [77] [Italics mine—C. L.]

Going into more detail, Marx asserts: "The sum total of these relations of production constitutes the economic structure of society—the real foundation, on which rise legal and political superstructures and to which correspond definite forms of social consciousness. The mode of production in material life determines the general character of the social, political and spiritual processes of life. *It is not the consciousness of men that determines their existence, but, on the contrary, their social existence determines their consciousness.*" [78] [Italics mine—C. L.] And Marx and Engels agree that "Morality, religion, metaphysics, all the rest of ideology and their corresponding forms of consciousness, thus no longer retain the semblance of independence." [79]

In correspondence towards the end of his life, Engels modified his economic determinism to a considerable degree. He says in a letter to Hans Starkenburg in 1894: "Political, juridical, philosophical, religious, literary, artistic, etc., development is based on economic development. But all these react upon one another and also upon the economic base. It is not that the economic position is the *cause and alone active*, while everything else only has a passive effect. There is, rather, interaction on the basis of the economic necessity, which *ultimately* always asserts itself. . . . Men make their history themselves, only in given surroundings which condition it and on the basis cf actual relations already existing, among which the economic relations, however much they may be influenced by the other political and ideological ones, are still ultimately the decisive ones, forming the red thread which runs through them and alone leads to understanding." [80]

This passage from Engels distinctly shows, it seems to me, that he was none too clear about the theory of economic determinism. In his letters he keeps repeating that economic factors are *ultimately* or *in the last analysis* decisive, but he does not give concrete temporal meaning to "ultimately" or state at what point or points in history "the last analysis" is actualized. Furthermore, Engels does not succeed in integrating his economic determinism with his acknowledgment that contingency is real. The inconsistencies and vagueness in the Marx-Engels doctrine have not been dispelled, so far as I know, by any Marxist economist, historian or philosopher in the Soviet Union, Communist China or anywhere else since the Russian Revolution of 1917. To say the least, there is a certain indeterminateness about Marxist determinism.

It has been suggested that when in *The Communist Manifesto* Marx and Engels called the triumph of the working class "inevitable," they were using the term in a hortatory or rhetorical sense to express unyielding determination and to boost the morale of the workers. However that may be, Communists throughout the world, and especially since 1917, have taken the inevitability theory very seriously. Lenin believed in it and Soviet leaders, particularly Nikita Khrushchev, have repeatedly stressed it in their public pronouncements.

Social scientists, whether Marxist or otherwise, may be able to discern clear trends in the realm of economic, political and social affairs; and in principle we must grant that such scientists are capable of discovering if-then laws in which the *then* factor will normally follow the occurrence of the *if* factor. But certainly no such law has yet been established as true in reference to large-scale national events such as proletarian revolutions that abolish capitalism and usher in a new socialist order. And even if such a law were in existence, the actualization of the *then* factor would not be inevitable because it might be prevented by the fortuitous intrusion of some large event.* Such a possibility must be taken into consideration even if the chance of its occurring is as slight as one in a million. In the turbulent international situation that confronts the world today, there could conceivably take place a disastrous nuclear war that would put an end to both capitalism and socialism everywhere.

It is irrefutable that economic forces and relations are of enormous consequence in affecting the course of human affairs. We must always remain indebted to Marx for having so forcefully called this fact to the attention of mankind. The real question is how far it is reasonable to push an economic interpretation of history. Perhaps both Marxists and non-Marxists will eventually be able to agree that economic factors are the *most* important in historical causation, but by no means all-determining.

We must regard with skepticism any theory of history that relies on *unicausal* or monistic explanation. In my judgment, allowance must be made, not only for the pervasive phenomena of chance and freedom of choice, but also for events of decisive importance that do not belong in

* Cf. p. 50.

the category of economics. Such was the sudden death of President Roosevelt in April 1945 owing to physical factors. That untoward occurrence had distressing and far-reaching effects on the domestic and foreign policies of the American Government.

In addition, it has been repeatedly established that individuals exercising freedom of choice can rise above their economic conditioning and monetary self-interest. Time and again men and women dedicated to some compelling ideal have shown a disregard for economic security, connubial bliss, domestic comfort, social prestige and life itself. Among the ideals I have in mind is the uncompromising determination to find and express the truth, no matter how injurious or even fatal the personal consequences may be.

Most pertinent here are the remarks made by Brand Blanshard, Professor Emeritus of Philosophy at Yale University, concerning both Marxist and Freudian theories of motivation: "There are such things after all as native intelligence and the pressure of evidence, and neither singly nor in combination are they the functions of anything economic. Indeed, as has often been pointed out, the very success of Marx or Freud in showing his theory true would render the theory itself incredible. If all philosophical theories are produced not by the pressure of evidence, but by irrelevant pushes and pulls, this theory itself must be so produced, and then why believe it? On the other hand, if the theory *has* been arrived at under the constraint of logic and facts, then there is no reason why other conclusions should not be arrived at in the same way, and the theory fails again.

"It may be suggested that the theory of Freud is more plausible than that of Marx because desire is more intimately bound up with thought than are economic conditions. Agreed. But the Freudian theory would hold only if the course of thought were under the complete control of some desire other than the desire for truth itself. Now the desire for truth may be more commonly diverted from its aim by these other desires than was realized before Freud wrote. But that intelligence never succeeds in following an argument where it leads, that it is invariably put off the scent by the seductions of some irrelevant desire seems to me false, and self-evidently false. And if it is, we must admit that intellectual insight is an independent factor which is neither an economic nor a psychological puppet." [81]

John Dewey, interpreting the thought of another leading philosopher, Morris R. Cohen, has generalized the principle of contingency for the scientific enterprise as a whole: "Science is bound to assume, no matter how far back it goes, a given distribution of material particles for which no reason can be assigned; these are just brutely so and so; moreover, all scientific explanation is selective; laws must limit themselves to a small number of variables; and this fact is identical with recognition that for law (and the sum of laws) facts excluded as irrelevant are contingent. Finally, laws themselves have contingency. We can carry back laws to a more general law, but that more general law has undemonstrable terms. In fact, the more general the law, the less deducible, by truism, are its terms. Contingency is final because things in the universe have individuality, as well as having relations which are necessary, universal and invariant." [82]

In stating that for law "facts excluded as irrelevant are contingent," Professor Dewey means that any if-then sequence or relation is operative only within some determinate system and that events taking place outside that system are contingent in relation to the law in question. When Dewey says that "things in the universe have individuality," he means that individuality, like contingency, is a metaphysical ultimate. Individuality in this sense signifies that every existent in the universe is a distinct individual, set off in its discreteness and particularity from all other entities and possessing an irreducible character of its own. Every object and event, then, is unique; and that uniqueness not only rules out determinism as all-governing, but is congruent with contingency as a generic trait of Nature.

Dewey shows that the operation of natural law is perfectly consistent with individuality: "In the description of causal sequences, we still have to start with and from existences, things that are individually and uniquely just what they are. The fact that we can reduce changes that occur to certain uniformities and regularities does not eliminate this original element of individuality, of preference and bias. On the contrary, the statement of laws presupposes just this capacity. We cannot escape this fact by an attempt to treat each thing as an effect of other things. That merely pushes individuality back into those other things. Since we have to admit individuality no matter how far we carry the chase, we might as well forego the labor and start with the unescapable fact.

"In short, anything that is has something unique in itself, and this unique something, enters into what it does. Science does not concern itself with the individualities of things. It is concerned with their *relations*. A law or statement of uniformity like that of the so-called causal sequence tells us nothing about a thing inherently; it tells us only about an invariant relation sustained in behavior of that thing with that of other things. That this fact implies contingency as an ultimate and irreducible trait of existence is something too complicated to go into here." [83]

Again, to spell out Dewey's meaning, every entity, including man, has uniform and dependable relations with other entities, but in its individuality also possesses attributes or peculiarities that do not enter into such relations. The French philosopher, Charles B. Renouvier, as interpreted by George Boas, Professor Emeritus of the History of Philosophy at Johns Hopkins University, illuminates the situation: "Insofar as any being is unique, to that extent it is undetermined or self-determined. And insofar as it is identical with other beings, to that extent the homogeneity of its class accounts for the regularity of its behavior." [84] When the unique attributes of a thing—those attributes that are not homogeneous with the rest of its class—interact with other things, then and there we have contingency.

A human being is the most complex example of individuality of which we are aware. Each person is a marvelously intricate and balanced system of causation, natural law and singularities. A large proportion of his interactions with the external environment and his fellow men do not fit into the classification of regular and precise if-then sequences and relations. This is a major and enduring reason why the social sciences have not attained results as certain and successful as the physical sciences. And if every man possesses freedom of choice, the lag in the social sciences becomes even more understandable.

The existence of contingency and individuality goes hand in hand with pluralism—the idea that the universe is a Many—as opposed to monism—the idea that the universe is a One, a vast, unified totality. Traditionally, determinism and fatalism have been bound up with a monistic metaphysics. We speak loosely of the "universe" to designate the whole of existence, including the enormous network of galaxies stretching out into unending space. But when we come to analyze the matter closely, we find that the infinitely diverse world of Nature radiates from different centers, that it is a radical multiplicity ever stemming from a plurality of event-streams. This makes impossible the absolute necessity expounded by the deterministic religions and philosophies, and at the same time establishes pluralism as a metaphysical ultimate along with contingency and individuality.

As William James acutely says: "Things are 'with' one another in many ways, but nothing includes everything, or dominates over everything. The word 'and' trails along after every sentence. . . . The pluralistic world is thus more like a federal republic than like an empire or a kingdom. . . . Monism, on the other hand, insists that when you come down to reality as such, to the reality of realities, everything is present to *everything* else in one vast instantaneous co-implicated completeness—nothing can in *any* sense, functional or substantial, be really absent from anything else, all things interpenetrate and telescope together in the great total conflux." [85] Some philosophers have extended this notion so far as to claim that in the last analysis the whole universe is the cause of each event within it.

Throughout Nature complicated and far-reaching interrelationships exist, but there are also constant cross-currents and conflicting forces. To be sure, unities small or large are universal phenomena, but there is no all-encompassing, overarching unity. The different entities that make up the world enter temporarily into identifiable systems, but there is no one system that welds together all the subsystems. Most simultaneous events are causally independent of one another; they have not been part of one another's pasts. But in the deterministic "block-universe," as James calls it, all present happenings take place as if fused tightly together in a massive, monolithic wave-front.

While all material particles are related to one another in respect to gravity, most of them are totally unrelated at any one time to most others in most ways. On the other hand, no entity is independent of all other entities. Every individual object has relations with other objects; events overlap, tangle with one another, intermesh like the teeth of a cogwheel. Relationships greatly vary. As Dewey puts it: "Some things are relatively insulated from the influence of other things; some things are easily invaded by others; some things are fiercely attracted to conjoin their activities with those of others. Experience exhibits every kind of connexion from the most intimate to mere external juxtaposition." [86]

A common feature of the classic deterministic monisms has been the denial or derogation of change and becoming, which are essential elements in a world where contingency and freedom of choice are real. The ancient Greek philosopher, Parmenides, was the first thinker in the West to formulate systematically the idea of all existence "as a single, timeless and indivisible Being whose perfection is precisely due to its immutability. For every change was conceived as a corruption unworthy of pure and perfect Being." [87] The great Sphere or One of Parmenides has exercised an immense and pervasive influence on philosophy and theology right down to the present day.

A last-ditch argument against the existence of objective contingency is that if there were an all-knowing mind in the universe or observing the universe, that mind could predict, from its knowledge of the complete state of affairs throughout the cosmos at any moment, everything that would happen anywhere, including the thoughts and actions of human beings, for all future time. The first philosopher to advance this theory was Gottfried Wilhelm Leibniz, a German of the seventeenth century.

Leibniz writes: "That everything is brought forth through an established destiny is just as certain as three times three is nine. For destiny consists in this, that everything is interconnected as in a chain and will as infallibly happen before it happens, as it infallibly happened after it happens. . . . Everything proceeds mathematically—that is, infallibly—in the whole wide world, so that if someone could have a sufficient insight into the inner parts of things, and in addition had remembrance and intelligence enough to consider all the circumstances and to take them into account, he would be a prophet and would see the future in the present as in a mirror." [88]

Early in the nineteenth century, a French astronomer and mathematician, the Marquis de Laplace, formulated Leibniz's idea more precisely: "An intelligent being who, at a given instant, knew all the forces animating nature and the relative position of the beings within it, would, if his intelligence were sufficiently capacious to understand these data, include in a single formula the movements of the largest bodies of the universe and those of its slightest atoms. Nothing would be uncertain to him; the future as well as the past would be present to his eyes." [89] The all-knowing Laplacean mind would be able to reconstruct the past of the universe by working backwards from effects to causes.*

On the face of it, Laplace's reasoning has an air of plausibility, but it is fallacious and circular in that the very assumption of a mind capable of conceiving everything, down to the last detail throughout the entire future, amounts to an assumption of the deterministic, anti-chance thesis that has to be proved. Such an intelligence could have an all-embracing preview of the future only if all existing entities could be counted on to produce cause-effect sequences that swept unendingly ahead in tight uniformities undis-

---

* Theoretically, "determinism read backwards is true—that is, the present does fully determine, in the sense of logically imply, the past." (Charles Hartshorne, *Beyond Humanism*, p. 138.)

90

turbed by any chance encounters or deviations. The existence of a Supreme Mind, then, or a Superscientist capable of infinite knowledge inclusive of the future, definitely implies universal determinism. Hence, anyone who believes in human freedom of choice must, if he is consistent, reject credence in the omniscient, prescient gods of traditional supernaturalism.

A strange fatalistic note creeps into some forms of Christianity that are not, like Calvinism, deterministic in essence. Thus God with overtones of determinism appears in the well-known Protestant burial service that quotes from the Book of Job: "The Lord gave, and the Lord hath taken away; blessed be the name of the Lord." And sometimes death notices begin: "Whereas God in his infinite wisdom has taken our dearly beloved. . . ." Without doubt some people are consoled by thinking that the loss of a loved one has been decreed, for some inscrutable reason, by a deterministic Divine Providence.

God as First Cause is another conception that paves the way for cosmic determinism. For in that mode he provides the one, mighty, initiating cause from which automatically flow all subsequent causes and effects. An altogether material phenomenon as First Cause would have the same necessitarian result. The pluralistic view I have outlined holds that if ever there was a beginning to the universe, which is most doubtful, it would have been beginnings, that is, a multitude of first causes all popping at once.

Curiously enough, God is frequently assigned responsibility for some happenings that are obviously due to contingency, as when some unusual, sudden, unexpected and violent manifestation of Nature results in death to human beings or destruction of their property. Indeed, such fortuitous calamities are explicitly classified as "Acts of God" in Anglo-American law and their occurrence exempts shipowners, for example, from legal liability for loss of life and property. This same exemption holds in regard to other common carriers, to insurance companies and in many other fields of law.

From time to time when actresses have unexpectedly become pregnant, they have claimed contractual immunity under the Act of God principle; but the courts have ruled that God was not involved in such cases.[90]

Are there any scientific findings that in themselves prove the presence of contingency in the cosmos? Numerous believers in freedom of choice have argued that Werner Heisenberg's work in quantum physics provides such proof. In 1927 Heisenberg established that it was impossible simultaneously to measure accurately *both* the position and the velocity of an electron. Since this means that a physicist cannot determine at any given moment where an electron will be at the next moment, Heisenberg called his discovery "the principle of uncertainty."

In philosophic and scientific circles a continuing debate has taken place as to the full meaning of this principle of uncertainty. Does it merely imply that physicists have not yet developed, and may never do so, instruments capable of making the dual measurements involved? Or does the principle connote that contingency applies to the activity of sub-atomic particles and therefore exists in the innermost heart of Nature? While I believe that contingency *is* operative in the sub-atomic world, I am not sure that Heisenberg's experiments clearly prove that fact.

According to Professor Čapek, however, the observation of radioactive phenomena, in the form of nuclear alpha particles, *does* prove objectively the existence of contingency. These particles, he argues, display random fluctuations in their behavior. He then states: "There is no intervention of an observer in the case of radioactive explosions which occur spontaneously and independently of any extranuclear factors. The function of the human observer here is passive; it is reduced to counting particles in a certain interval of time and measuring their energy *after* their emergence from the nucleus. It is true that even this apparently passive role means an intervention in the observed physical process; thus the counting of the emitted particles is impossible without using a spinthariscope or Geiger counter, and to these observational procedures everything which Heisenberg stated in his original formulation of the principle applies. But this intervention does obviously occur *after* the event, that is, *after* the radioactive explosion has taken place. Thus the uncertainty of the radioactive disintegrations is independent of the limitations of human experimental technique; the term 'indeterminacy' or 'contingency' is far more appropriate and much less misleading than 'uncertainty.' " [91]

Equally relevant for indicating that contingency exists in the nature of things is that "the physicists themselves suggest that even the patent regularities are a statistical mass phenomenon summing up vast numbers of more or less lawless atomic events." [92] Those events taken singly do not fit into any fixed pattern. It may be added that science's increasing reliance on an ultimate probabilism* points to more than subjective uncertainty on the part of investigators and suggests a metaphysical status for contingency. But if universal determinism is valid, then every event is inevitable precisely as it happens and the whole notion of probability becomes self-contradictory. For if everything that is exists necessarily and there can be no middle ground between necessity and impossibility, how can anything be merely probable?

The scientific study of probability has recently extended to games of chance. Says Alfred Landé, Professor of Physics at Ohio State University: ". . . determinism does not and never will make sense, in particular when applied to those random-like situations we know from games of chance. The question is, of course, whether there are true games of chance, i.e., random-like situations that are irreducible to concealed causes *in principle*. In this argument about principles it makes little difference whether the random-like situations are those encountered in atomic experiments, in dice games, or in the games insurance companies play with their clients." [93]

Professor Landé cites experiments with a game of balls dropped through a chute onto a sharp or slightly rounded knife edge. Almost all the balls will fall to the right or left of the knife in accordance with the mechanically set angle of the aim. "Experience shows, however, that

* Cf. pp. 50-51.

between right- and left-hand aim there is always a small but *finite* range $\triangle a$ of aim within which an experimentally adjusted angle *a* leads neither to all balls dropping to the right nor to all balls dropping to the left but rather to both r-and l-balls occurring at a certain frequency ratio. The latter varies from 100 : 0 to 0 : 100 when the aim is shifted from the right to the left of the small range $\triangle a$." [94] Landé concludes that this fluctuation of the balls cannot be properly explained on a deterministic basis and that such games of chance demonstrate contingency as an irreducible trait of Nature.

As a counter-weight to all arguments for the existence of objective chance, determinists are likely to point to the Law of Parsimony. This important scientific law, sometimes known as Ockham's Razor, states that in explaining any phenomenon or phenomena we must depend on the fewest number of assumptions that are necessary to account adequately for all the facts involved. There is no doubt that universal determinism fulfils the ideal of simplicity of hypothesis by its doctrine that necessity, through the omnipresent flow of cause and effect, rules the totality of existence, including all forms of life. The Law of Parsimony, however, cannot save the determinist thesis, because that thesis does *not* "account for all the facts involved." It does not account for the complicating facts of contingency, individuality, potentiality and human freedom.

It is a constant temptation for philosophers and scientists to advance theories that oversimplify the behavior of things, and thus misuse the Law of Parsimony. In so doing they commit "the reductive fallacy" of trying to con-

jure away the vast complexity of the cosmos by illegiti-
mately classifying certain multiple phenomena under one
large category. This is precisely what the determinists do.

Anti-determinists would be guilty of this same fallacy
if they countered the idea of absolute determinism with the
idea of absolute chance. To accept such a theory would indeed imply "the suicide of reason." For absolute chance
would mean the total absence of law and a world in which
universal chaos prevailed. No intelligent believer in freedom of choice adheres to this untenable position. Always
we come back to the empirically established truth that both
necessity and contingency are cosmic ultimates.*

* It is curious that so many current discussions of the free
choice issue give little or no attention to the question of chance or
contingency. In two valuable symposia published in 1966—*Freedom and Determinism*, edited by Professor Keith Lehrer, and *Free
Will and Determinism*, edited by Dr. Bernard Berofsky—there is
virtually no discussion of contingency. Since freedom of choice is
obviously an impossibility unless contingency objectively exists in
Nature, it seems to me that these two books are lacking in depth.

PART TWO

4

The Role of Potentiality
and Deliberation

According to the determinist analysis, when a man is choosing between two or more alternatives, his final choice is all settled in advance, completely necessitated by the course of Nature from aeons past. In short, for the determinist, alternatives and potentiality are, like contingency, mere illusions in the human mind; not only everything that happens is fated to occur, but everything that does not happen is fated not to occur. In this way the concept of cosmic determinism robs potentiality of its essential meaning by reading back present actuality into the primordial flux; by declaring that at any one moment in the history of the universe every future event is then and there somehow contained or implied. Thus there has existed only one universal potentiality throughout all time, namely the potentiality of the one actuality that inevitably occurs. For determinism there are no plural or alternate possibilities; each thing, and things as a whole, have only one possible line of development. Unrealized possibilities, all the haunting might-have-been's of history and personal life, are illusory. The present unfolds from the past, and the future from the present, as automatically as a motion picture projected onto the screen from a roll of film.

I reject this interpretation of the world. The presence of chance or contingency decisively undermines the determinist position and ensures the existence of potentiality and different alternatives. Potentiality in this plural sense is, as Aristotle taught, a fundamental metaphysical trait, signifying that every existing object has certain inherent possibilities of activity, adaptability, interaction, change and development. Precisely which potentiality or potentialities are realized depends on the impinging forces, often including human agency, that interact with the entity in question.

The late Professor Frederick J. E. Woodbridge, one of Columbia University's most distinguished philosophers, specifies what those "impinging forces" accomplish: "We may recognize at once that the bare potential contains within itself no elements which can lead to its own realization. To be more than a mere possibility, something else must supervene. The whole of existence at any moment faces the future, therefore, with untold possibilities. Each of them, if started on the road toward realization, has its path determined, but from the point of view of potentiality, all are equally possible. The determined path presents us with all the elements of a necessary connection, but we look in vain for such connection when we seek among the untold possibilities the one which is in effect to be.

"Something new must add itself, must emerge, as it

were, out of non-existence into being. An arbitrary point of departure must arise, and when once it has arisen, the movement proceeds with definiteness. It is thus, whether we like it or not, that the doctrine of chance originates. To adopt again the argument of Aristotle, the elimination of chance is the elimination of the potential. For if there had always existed the elements necessary to transform the potential, it would have always been transformed, and so motion and alteration could have no place in the scheme of things." [95]

Professor Lamprecht outlines the implications of potentiality for freedom of choice: "The plural potentialities of nature are the significant basis of human choice. It is insufficient to argue that because things are as they are they will be as they will be. Rather, because things are as they are, an agent who imaginatively foresees the diverse potentialities of things may choose freely within given limits. Freedom is never total—it is not freedom *from* the world. But it is genuine—it is freedom *within* the world. There is at least no supernatural agency introduced into a mechanical nature in order to give man freedom at the expense of nature's laws." [96]

"Stones, plants, even most animals are not free. They react only to the actuality that forces itself upon them with insistent pressure. Man is supreme among the products of nature just because in imagination disciplined by stern experience, he can look through the actual to the potential, can respond to the actual in the light of the potential, *can choose between the contingent factors of nature.* Freedom is perhaps the latest development of a basic trait of nature; it is latest in time but supreme in importance. It is late because its appearance is consequent to the prior development of memory, imagination, knowledge. But even this latest development was latent in nature from the start, waiting for such a creature as man to enter through its possession into mastery over the rest of nature. Freedom is, then, the exploitation of nature's contingency." [97] [Italics mine—C. L.]

Let us consider the various potentialities for man inherent in a tall tree that has been cut down for commercial uses. We can use the timber to build boats; we can use it for constructing a bridge; we can saw it into boards; we can cut it into small pieces for firewood; we can manufacture tables from it; we can carve statuettes from it; we can fashion salad bowls from it; we can produce book-cases from it; we can make skis from it; we can utilize the timber for erecting a house; and so on.

Here we have ten obvious possibilities for the final utilization of the tree; and for each of the categories I have mentioned there are numerous sub-possibilities. Scores of different sorts of houses, for instance, could be constructed from the wood. At the very least, then, the potentialities of the felled tree for human purposes total more than one hundred. It is my claim that man can freely choose to actualize any one of these potentialities. Were determinism true, the tree would possess only *one* potentiality—the one that happened to come to pass—and all the other potentialities would be illusory.

The dead tree lying on the ground or floating down a river to the lumber mill cannot determine what will eventually happen to it. Some active agency, human or otherwise, must intervene to make that determination. And one potentiality for the tree is that it will be turned into ashes by a raging fire in the mill before any man can put it to use. In this case, contingency again comes into play, since the event-stream constituted by the fire meets and wreaks havoc upon the event-stream constituted by the tree.

But if no fire takes place and man-as-cause deals with the tree in the mill, then a man is the independent event-stream that intersects with the tree as a separate event-stream. And he exercises freedom of choice by deciding which of the many potentialities of the tree he wishes to bring into being, thereby discarding any other possibilities. As Alfred N. Whitehead points out: "Whatever is realized in any one occasion of experience necessarily excludes the unbounded welter of contrary possibilities. There are always 'others' which might have been and are not." [98]

Many a time during pleasant summers among the off-shore islands of Maine my family and I have discussed plans to go on an all-day outing. Would it be a long sail with picnic lunch on one of the pink-white granite islands of Penobscot Bay, a climb up a mountain that has a wonderful view from the top, or a hike along some rugged shoreline? Those three alternatives were not the subjective creations of our minds; they were objective potentialities of Nature. The sea, the mountain and the shore were all there before we were born; and to say they represented three genuine possibilities for a day in the open air essentially implies that we had freedom of choice in our decision where to go.

Other potentialities were also present for an all-day

excursion: a trip southward by motorboat to visit Monhegan Island, a trip north to Mt. Desert Island to explore Acadia National Park, and a long sail around the large island of Vinalhaven. A man is not necessarily aware of *all* existing alternatives when he is deliberating about a choice; and the multiple possibilities that Nature is continually offering us exist concretely whether or not we give them conscious consideration.

It is the ever plural potentialities in the world and human life that give us the opportunity to make choices that count among alternatives that are real. However, possibilities, like human choices, are limited in scope. The healthiest acorn is not capable of growing into an apple tree; the most versatile horse does not have the ability, except in fairy tales, to fly through the air. The respective natures of every event, object and creature set deterministic bounds to their potentialities.

Now we return to the fundamental role of reason, intelligence, deliberation, in man's free choosing and shall see how the thinking process ties in with the existence of potentiality. Freedom of choice is of course intimately linked with the capacity for thought. Choosing means *to make up one's mind;* altering a choice means *to change one's mind.*

Human beings are able to make very rapid decisions, especially when habit patterns have been established, as in driving an automobile or in running a self-service elevator.* In general, however, men do not have to take action instantly when faced with a problem. They are not required,

* Cf. pp. 128-29.

like inanimate agents, to react in a speedy stimulus-response manner. They have time to glimpse imaginatively the various potentialities in the situation, to propose to themselves different hypothetical solutions and to work out in thought the logical consequences of each one.

It is this sort of deliberation "which decisively contrasts intelligent conduct or behavior with reflex, instinctive and habitual conduct or behavior—delayed reaction with immediate reaction." [99] In short, the enterprise of thinking, with its manipulation of ideas that symbolize things and events, enables human beings to stand aside temporarily from the flux of existence and think through the different options that are open to them. In regard to the more serious problems, the deliberative process may extend over weeks, months or even years. Whatever period of time is required, a man is able to hold in his memory the question at issue and the various factors involved.

At the same time there is a natural continuity between freedom of choice and the ways of even inanimate objects. In John Dewey's words: "Preferential action in the sense of selective behavior is a universal trait of all things, atoms and molecules as well as plants, animals and man. Existences, universally as far as we can tell, are cold and indifferent in the presence of some things and react energetically in either a positive or negative way to other things. These 'preferences' or differential responses of behavior, are due to their own constitution; they 'express' the nature of the things in question. . . .

"We may say that a stone has its preferential selections set by a relatively fixed, a rigidly set, structure and that no anticipation of the results of acting one way or another enter into the matter. The reverse is true of human action. In so far as a variable life-history and intelligent insight and foresight enter into it, choice signifies a capacity for deliberately changing preferences. . . . The fact that all things show bias, preference or selectivity of reaction, while not itself freedom, is an indispensable condition of any human freedom." [100]

Analyzing in depth the intellectual process which leads to a decision, we find that a man ordinarily employs *general* ideas or "universals" as they are called in philosophy. It is elementary that each general concept covers a number of particulars. Thus under the broad classification of *flower* there are hundreds of varieties. And if I wish to send my mother some flowers for her birthday, I can select from a number of possibilities at my neighborhood florist's. Deliberating in terms of general ideas proceeds on the basis that potentiality is real.

Professor Hartshorne develops the implications here: ". . . our very power to form general conceptions (in a sense in which these are beyond the reach of the other animals) is the same as our being not determined by irresistible impulse, habit or antecedent character, to but one mode of acting in a given case. The openness to alternatives, the flexibility, of our response is the behavioristic aspect of our knowledge of the universal, as that which can be indifferently instanced by this particular *or* by that. Such instancing, by its very meaning, must have wide ranges of freedom. Freedom in the indeterministic sense is thus inherent in rational understanding as such, understanding through universals." [101]

Hartshorne continues: "Universals cannot imply their instances, so that if there are universals there are non-deterministic relations between them and their instances. The universal is essentially an *indecision* between its instances; to say universals are real is to say indecision is real. A universal is . . . a 'determinable,' not a 'determinate.' 'Color' *may* be a red; it *may* be a green; it *need not* be either. Determinism finds no place for 'may be's'; hence it must deny universals altogether. This is a perfect refutation of determinism, for if a law is not a universal, what is it?" [102]

The formula for an established law or if-then sequence is a universal because it may be exemplified by many different particulars.* Regard, for example, the law (not including inner mechanisms) utilized in effecting telephone conversations: If you dial a certain number, you will be able to speak with the person you want or someone else who answers at the number called. This general formula, however, does not indicate what number or numbers you or anyone else will call. Thousands, even millions, of different numbers can be dialed, and to the ends of the earth. All of

---

* Cf. Professor Lamprecht: "Causal laws are universal propositions. And causal events . . . are, each of them, single, particular, individual. Each causal event would still be the causal event it empirically is, even if it were the only event of the kind that had ever occurred and could therefore never be grouped together with similar events under a comprehensive formula. Causal laws, of course, never cause anything: universal propositions do not act." *The Metaphysics of Naturalism,* p. 106.

them are possible instances of the law regulating phone calls.

The thinking of a student on entering college can serve as an illustration of Hartshorne's analysis of universals. "A good college education" is the general conception, the universal, in the student's mind as he starts to look through the catalogue of courses available at the institution where he has enrolled. Presumably there will be some required courses, but beyond those the student will need other courses to fill out his curriculum; and there will be a large number of possibilities for him to choose from. Because he has acquired a growing interest in art and history, he may select an optional course in one of those fields. His faculty advisor will give him wise counsel, friends in the upper classes will tell him who are the most stimulating teachers, and he may even remember what his parents recommended. At the beginning of every academic year he will go through much the same procedure, with added wisdom (we hope) from his widened experience. And at some point in his college career he will have to make the additional choice of a field of concentration.

The student's ability to think about the general idea of "a good college education," to explore mentally the many alternative courses that he can take, to obtain relevant information about them and finally to pick out the ones he judges most suitable for his purposes—all this is not mere play-acting for the selection of a curriculum that was predetermined in the genes of his forefathers. It is a serious exercise in deliberation that in itself all but implies freedom of choice.

Professor Keith Lehrer of the University of Rochester further elucidates our point when he states that ". . . adequate evidence for the belief that we have free will is the fact that we deliberate about future actions. When we deliberate about whether or not we shall perform some future action, we *must* be convinced that the action in question is in our power, that is, we must be convinced that it is up to us whether or not we shall perform the action. In order to deliberate about whether or not we shall perform some future action we must be convinced that we can choose to perform the action and also that we can choose not to perform it, for we cannot seriously deliberate about whether or not we shall perform an action unless we believe that we can choose whether or not we shall perform it." [103]

Of course free choice results in wrong decisions as well as right, in furthering the bad as well as the good, in lying as well as in telling the truth. Furthermore, in the process of studying the implications of different alternatives, ". . . no one can foresee all consequences because no one can be aware of all the conditions that enter into their production. Every person builds better or worse than he knows." [104] It is difficult, if not impossible, to anticipate all the by-products of conscious actions, usually projected into an intricate web of human and other relationships. Yet it remains true that the more a decision is informed by knowledge and guided by intelligence, the better it is likely to be.

In the *Dialogues* of Plato, Socrates argues that all men invariably choose to do what they think is best and that they must rely primarily on knowledge, discriminating between good and evil, to make that choice. If an individual knows what is good, he will surely choose it; if he knows what is bad, he will as certainly shun it. He may well make wrong choices, but that will be because he is pursuing only an apparent good and does not at that point possess the knowledge to see that it is really bad. Ignorance blinds him and binds him. This line of reasoning leads Socrates to his ultimate conclusion that virtue is knowledge, and vice ignorance. This lofty intellectualistic ethics is unsound because, as human experience obviously shows, the stronger emotions, desires or appetites, sometimes in the form of unconscious drives, often over-rule human reason and knowledge. That is why people drink themselves to death and over-eat into the grave.*

A major factor in wise choices is to know what is objectively possible and what impossible, what is fairly certain and what is faintly probable. For human freedom always operates within definite limits established by past and present circumstances. To this extent every human choice and action is partly subject to determinism. Man as a finite being with a specific physical structure can function and survive only if a number of environmental conditions are present. He will die if it is too hot or too cold, if all oxygen is cut off, if there is not sufficient food and drink. And he can act only when and where he happens to be, at a specific *now* in time and *here* in space. Yet with all the limitations inherent in his own being and the further bounds imposed by the external world, man does possess in general a great deal of freedom.

* Cf. pp. 151-52.

In this sense human life can aptly be compared, to take a cherished example, with chess. Players in this fascinating game are free to make an immense variety of moves, but they are limited by the recognized rules which are a necessary part of the game and which represent law or determinism; and they must also use certain instruments: the different sorts of chessmen. The same principles hold true for bridge, baseball, golf, tennis and croquet—indeed, for all competitive games and sports.

Economic, political and social conditions are of course very important in limiting the range of human freedom. Yet however circumscribing boundaries of this kind may be in a given situation, some leeway invariably remains for free choice. Even when confronted by a Hobson's choice, in which you must take what is offered or nothing, you have the freedom to choose the nothing. Dr. Viktor Frankl comments: "Certainly man is free, but he is not floating freely in airless space. He is always surrounded by a host of restrictions. These restrictions, however, are the jumping-off points for his freedom. Freedom presupposes restrictions, is contingent upon restrictions. . . . The ground on which a man walks is always being transcended in the process of walking, and serves as ground only to the extent that it is transcended, that it provides a springboard." [105]

Under an iron dictatorship the average citizen's range of organizational activities and free speech is far less than in a democracy. But regardless of the sort of political system prevailing in a country, there is one exceedingly significant moral choice a man can always make. He can defy the government. He can say, "No, I will not keep silent.

No, I will not obey." He can with set purpose choose the path to a concentration camp or even to death for the sake of his principles. Throughout history numberless individuals, remembered and unremembered, have given up their lives rather than give up their convictions. Some have even committed suicide, deliberately and rationally, as their ultimate protest against ruthless and bloody tyranny.

Dr. Frankl survived three years of imprisonment at Auschwitz and other Nazi extermination centers and describes his experiences in a soul-searing book, *Man's Search for Meaning*. He writes: "We who lived in concentration camps can remember the men who walked through the huts comforting others, giving away their last piece of bread. They may have been few in number, but they offer sufficient proof *that everything can be taken from a man but one thing: the last of the human freedoms—to choose one's attitude in any given circumstances, to choose one's own way.*

"And there were always choices to make. Every day, every hour, offered the opportunity to make a decision, a decision which determined whether you would or would not submit to those powers which threatened to rob you of your very self, your inner freedom; which determined whether or not you would become the plaything of circumstance, renouncing freedom and dignity to become molded into the form of the typical inmate. . . .

"In the final analysis it becomes clear that the sort of person the prisoner became was the result of an inner decision, and not the result of camp influences alone. Fundamentally, therefore, any man can, even under such circum-

stances, decide what shall become of him—mentally and
spiritually. He may retain his human dignity even in a concentration camp. Dostoievsky said once, 'There is only one
thing that I dread: not to be worthy of my sufferings.' These
words frequently came to mind after I became acquainted
with those martyrs whose behavior in camp, whose suffering
and death, bore witness to the fact that the last inner freedom cannot be lost." [106] [Italics mine—C. L.]

Some hard-core determinists have adopted the theory
of epiphenomenalism, which holds that consciousness,
thought and psychological states in general are mere by-
products of neural processes in the brain and possess no
causal or practical efficacy. From this standpoint man's
consciousness plays the role of a passive spectator watching,
enjoying, suffering the unfolding of inescapable destiny.
"The view of psychological states as 'epiphenomena'—
events accompanying but not making any difference to
physiological processes—is difficult to reconcile with evolu-
tionary theory. For such epiphenomenal states would be
useless to the organisms which manifested them and should
therefore have atrophied and disappeared long ago, instead
of increasing in number and complexity as they clearly
have." [107] Thus, epiphenomenalism not only makes a mys-
tery out of the evolution of mind, but also de-naturalizes it
by denying that thinking can have any effect in and upon
the physical world, including the human body.

The more persuasive determinists, however, admit

that thinking plays a special role in the mechanism of choice, but insist that the whole process of intellectually weighing different solutions to a problem is deterministic because thought itself must obey the cause-effect patterns already established in the brain. Those inescapable patterns have been built up in each individual by his entire education and experience in interaction with the native biological inheritance handed down to him by parents, grandparents and ancestors *ad infinitum*. If a man produces a genuinely new idea, that also follows from causal necessities in the cerebral cortex. In this view human volition is simply the dynamic urge to carry out wishes and ideas that have become part of our being through the impact of strict causation both within us and from outside us.

True freedom, from this standpoint, is the capacity for acting according to one's true character, to be altogether *self*-determined and not subject to external coercion. As Gardner Williams puts it, "Preference plus power contain the essence of freedom." [108] This doctrine deserves careful consideration owing to the care and consistency with which it has been formulated. Some of the West's most noted philosophers—Spinoza and others—have supported it.

But the formula that Professor Williams suggests can be applied to living organisms in general. Animals, for instance, are endowed with a considerable degree of spontaneity and are able most of the time to act according to their inherent nature, without compulsion or interference from extraneous forces. In truth, though Professor Williams and his fellow determinists grant that freedom for human beings is far wider in scope than for any other organic species, they ascribe to man no greater intrinsic autonomy than to a toad, a turtle or a turtle-dove.

Relevant here is a statement by the late Jerome Frank, the brilliant lawyer and Federal judge, in his book *Fate and Freedom:* "Some determinists seek to avoid the problem of human freedom by this ingenious argument: Often, they say, a man's external surroundings present him with several real alternative courses of conduct; those surroundings themselves do not constrain him to choose any particular one of those alternatives; his objectives and motives, the products of his personality—the kind of person he is—determine his choice; in that sense he is free, unconstrained, because he acts of his own volition within the range of the external alternatives open to him. But this argument glosses over the basic issue. For, according to determinists, rigid causation, with never the tiniest escape from it, operated at every second in the development of the man's personality, shaping inexorably his objectives, his motives, his volition; his choice merely seems real to him because, at the instant of decision, he is ignorant of the past and present facts which render his decision compulsory." [109]

Judge Frank goes on to say that when the determinists assert that the individual's self or personality plays an important part in a decision "they are being disingenuous. For, if their causality doctrine is sound, the man is what he is at the moment of decision because his immediately preceding past, itself inflexibly determined, so dictated; a similar inflexible dictation directed his heredity . . . as well as his environment and the past of that environment. . . . As, then, according to their doctrine, the man cannot help choosing exactly as he does, the determinists' picture of the freedom of human choice is the picture of an illusion." [110]

The orthodox determinist constantly proclaims that science and its methods strongly support his viewpoint. Professor Abraham Wolf, late of the University of London, exposes this contention: "In a world of thorough-going determinism, in which all things were mechanically or quasi-mechanically predetermined, in which even men of science were not free to think as they thought fit in the light of the evidence before them, how could science lay any claim to truth, universally valid truth? There could be nothing but individual opinion, the opinion of each individual being as necessary, and probably as far from the truth, as that of any other. It may be, of course, that our world is such a world. But in such a world there could be no science. And to insist upon maintaining such a deterministic view of the world in the name, and on behalf of, science, is simply to stultify oneself." [111]

Morris Ginsberg, Professor Emeritus of Sociology at the London School of Economics, further develops this line of thought, declaring that determinism, if true, would nullify scientific method: "If it be maintained that a man's judgments are themselves completely determined, that he cannot help making the judgments he makes, the answer is that this makes nonsense of all knowledge. . . . If all judgments were causally necessitated, they would all be on the same level and it would be impossible to distinguish some as true and others as false. Sense and nonsense would all be equally necessitated. The whole notion of going by the evidence would lose all its meaning, if in forming a judgment we were completely unable to resist the violence of present desire, the effects of past habits, the persistence of ancient prejudices or the forces of the unconscious." [112]

Professor Alburey Castell of the College of Wooster carries on the argument: "Are we to say that a mental process is trustworthy simply because each stage is causally necessitated by what precedes it? If so, the processes of a sick or crazed or over-fatigued mind are as trustworthy as the processes of a healthy, alert, sensitized mind, since in both cases (the claim is) each stage is causally necessitated by what precedes it. But if the processes of a sane mind are no more trustworthy than the processes of an insane mind, why do we trust the man who reasons in support of the theory that no one ever could do other than he does do? His reasoning processes are no more binding than a series of hiccoughs." [113]

Following through the implications of Professor Castell's statement, we see that determinism is logically self-defeating. For when the determinist propounds his theory, argues insistently in its favor and rebuts the free choice doctrine, he is all the while implicitly affirming that he has responsibly adopted his thesis and that thus he has chosen freely between true and false. If, as Professor Paul Weiss of Yale University shows, the determinist "denies that he freely considers and responsibly adopts his position, he denies that he has a view that opposes others; his view is then acknowledged to be but one verbal fact among a multitude, no better or worse, no more or less important, than any other." [114]

Professor Weiss lays it on the line: "The statement that this was a deterministic world and the statement that it was not would, for a comprehensive determinism, be on a level, equally true and equally false, and therefore— since truth and falsehood are mutually exclusive—really incapable of either truth or falsehood. . . . A deterministic world is one in which the deterministic thesis could not be offered as true because such a world allows no place for beings who are responsible for asserting truths." [115]

When an individual is reasoning his way to the solution of a problem, to the truth as he sees it, he continually discards the ideas he thinks false and accepts those he deems true. Freedom of choice predominates in both the rejection and acceptance of ideas; and we see again that this freedom is essential to the search for and discovery of the truth.

An expert in psychotherapy, Professor Carl A. Rogers, presents a trenchant critique of those who interpret science as proving determinism. He offers two main points:

"1. In any scientific endeavor—whether 'pure' or applied science—there is a prior personal subjective choice of the purpose or value which that scientific work is perceived as serving.

"2. This subjective value choice which brings the scientific endeavor into being must always lie outside of that endeavor, and can never become a part of the science involved in that endeavor. . . .

"We must recall that science itself, and each specific scientific endeavor, each change of course in a scientific research, each interpretation of the meaning of a scientific finding and each decision as to how the finding shall be applied, rests upon a personal subjective choice. . . . A personal subjective choice made by man sets in motion the operations of science, which in time proclaims that there can be no such thing as a personal subjective choice." [116]

When a man carefully deliberates about a problem, he will consider various reasons for adopting this solution or that. Whatever the origin of those reasons, whether in his own experience or from some external source, they do not have a dynamic existence of their own that can deterministically push a person to select one alternative or another; they do not sway him until he incorporates them into his own thinking. In brief, the reasons do not choose you; you choose the reasons that seem the most convincing, after freely assessing the pros and cons. This is what reasoning means and what reliance on reason entails.

Professor Emeritus of Philosophy Raphael Demos of Harvard University elucidates: "I submit that necessitation by reason is no less determination than necessitation by appetite. . . . Reason recognizes the moral law and respects it; appetite aims at pleasure. Yet, in fact, moral choice is a choice between reason and appetite. By identifying the self with reason, both Plato and Kant make freedom impossible, no less than Hume and John Stuart Mill do, who identify the self with appetite. To repeat—the situation of ethical choice is one in which the agent decides whether to follow reason or desire. . . ." [117]

When analyzing *ex post facto* why a man has chosen alternative *a* instead of alternative *b*, the determinist may point to the reasons and say, "See, those reasons necessi-

tated the person's choice and no other course was possible."
Professor F. C. S. Schiller, the Oxford don, exposes this
fallacy when he says: "The alternative, had it been adopted,
would have seemed equally intelligible, just because it was
such as to be really entertained by the agent under the circumstances, and as naturally rooted in them." [118] And
Schiller asks, "Does it not follow . . . that *whichever of
the alternatives is chosen, it will appear to be rationally
connected with the antecedent circumstances?*" [119] The answer of course is Yes.

Determinists are prone to seize upon this fact as a
confirmation of their position. But it demonstrates just the
opposite, namely, that we always have a plurality of intelligible possibilities from which we can select. This is true
even if only two decisions—to do or not to do something—
are relevant. After the event, the actual choice—which is a
contingent happening—can to a great extent be rationally
explained, just as can contingent conjunctions and events
in Nature at large. This is why psychiatrists and psychoanalysts are quite successful in satisfactorily relating a patient's present to his past, but much less successful in pre-
dicting his future behavior from his present behavior. [120]

The fundamental mistake of the determinist in his
analysis of thinking and choosing is to treat them primarily
as items in the *history* of an individual, to describe these
activities as if they were fully completed episodes of the
departed past instead of functions of the living present. As
Henri Bergson points out, the determinist reaches his conclusion by analyzing the phenomenon of human choice *as
already made, not as in the making.*

Professor Weiss sums up this phase of our argument: "The contention that men are determined and the contention that they are free seem opposed. They are not. Determinism applies to what has happened when all the conditions are already present and fulfilled. Freedom applies to what is happening and will happen; it concerns the creation of new conditions and thus of consequences that until then have not been necessitated." [121]

5
Causation and Free Choice

A potent reason for the widespread acceptance of the determinist thesis is a rather common misunderstanding of the operation of cause and effect. Many individuals, including scientists and philosophers, look upon the present as merely the effect of antecedent causes and forget that the present in its multitudinous forms is itself an active cause, the spearhead of all existence and activity, the great forward thrust of universal being. The past does not create the present; it is always the activity of some immediate present that produces the past, working upon it, transforming it or conserving what has been built by *former* presents that have become part of the past. The present alone exists and has efficacy; the past is efficacious only as embodied in the substance or structure of some present event or object. As the dynamic present forges ahead, it leaves its past behind it, making a trail as it were, as a skier gliding downhill through the snow or a boat stirring up a foamy wake.

Nature in its every mode—the whole vast aggregate of inanimate matter, the swarming profusion of earthly life, man in his every aspect—exists only as an event or events taking place at this instant moment which is now. To exist means universally to be a form or quality of activity in some temporal present. Whatever exists must possess immediacy.

The activity which took place in the past built the foundations upon which the immediate present operates. What happened in the past establishes many limitations as well as potentialities; it always conditions present activity, and present activity conditions the events of the future. But conditioning is not the same as total determination. In other words, *the antecedents of a present activity provide the necessary, but not the only or sufficient, conditions for it.* Each day's present, in its creative onward sweep, brings into being fresh patterns of existence, maintains other patterns and destroys still others.

Professor Čapek gets to the heart of the matter when, speaking of *"a really growing world with genuine novelties emerging from past antecedents,"* he states: "In such a growing world every present event is undoubtedly caused, though not necessitated, by its own past. For, as long as it is not yet present, its specific character remains uncertain for one simple reason: that it is only its presentness which creates its specificity, i.e., brings an end to its uncertainty by eliminating all other possible features incompatible with it. Thus every present event is by its own essence *an act of selection* ending the hesitation of reality between various possibilities. The terms 'selection' and 'hesitation' appear to be metaphorical and even anthropomorphic at first glance; in truth they express nothing but the ambiguous character of the unrealized future as well as its subsequent concrete realization. They describe complementary aspects of every temporal process: its indeterminacy and its creative character." [122]

Active, thinking, choosing men, together with those natural forces under their control, are an unceasing *wave of the present*. This creative present, however conditioned and restricted by the effects of previous presents, possesses genuine initiative; as it moves forward, it pushes into the past the transformations it makes in the malleable substance of the already existent. Professor Woodbridge clarifies the issue: "The past is not the cause or beginning of the present, but the effect and result of history; so that every historical thing leaves, as it were, its past behind it as the record of its life in time. . . . Everything that grows or changes manufactures a past by realizing a future. . . . Each career is the producer, but not the product of its past." [123]

It is easy to become confused about the meaning of past and future. Since neither of them exist in the present, they are both imaginative concepts. They assume, however, the status of concrete present existence upon our calendars where time is represented visually in terms of space and therefore *mis*represented. The ordinary calendar preserves the old notion of the world as being *in* time and moving through it. We know, on the contrary, that time is a quality of activity or process, a relationship between events.

Professor Woodbridge gives a convincing critique of

philosophies that in effect make the spatialization of time a central tenet: "Whatever happens is . . . conceived to be the effect of what has already happened, rather than the active conservation and working over of what has already happened. The past is made the cause and producer of the present, so that the state of the world at any moment is only the result or outcome of what it was in the preceding moment. Today is thought to be the effect of yesterday and the cause of tomorrow, and is thus but a transition from one day to another. Time-processes are thus robbed of any genuine activity or productivity, and time itself is made to be nothing but the sequential order in which events occur. . . .

"Time is not like a line already drawn. It is more like a line in the drawing. You take the pencil and the line is left behind it as the pencil moves. New points are being constantly added to what has gone before. The line is being manufactured. . . . The line, instead of growing into the future, grows into the past—continually as more and more of it is drawn." [124] [Italics mine—C. L.]

We now turn to the distinction, crucial for our discussion, between the existing subject matter—what Aristotle called the material cause—and the agent or force that acts upon it—what Aristotle called the *efficient cause.** To quote Professor Lamprecht again: "Subject-matter and agency are both actualities of the present. But their roles are different. The former is that which is acted upon; the latter is that which acts. That which is acted upon may well

---

* In his philosophy Aristotle distinguished four different kinds of cause. *Efficient cause* in his terminology has come to mean plain *cause* in modern usage.

also be agent, because the interactions of nature are highly complicated. And that which acts may also be subject-matter for some other agent. We cannot, therefore, pick out any actuality of the present and regard it as either subject-matter or as agent in any absolute sense. . . .

"A physician who heals is agent and his patient is subject-matter, even though, simultaneously with the healing activity of the physician, the patient also acts in various ways upon the physician. The wind is agent and the bending elm is subject-matter, even though, simultaneously with the impact of the wind on the tree, the elm diverts the wind somewhat from the course it would, in the absence of the elm at just that spot, have taken. But the physician and the wind, in their roles as agents, are not subject-matter; and the patient and the elm, in their roles as subject-matter, are not agents. The distinction between subject-matter and agent is absolute, even if the actualities to which the distinction can be applied are complexly interrelated and continually changing in those interrelations." [125]

This distinction holds for a human agent putting into effect a present choice that affects his own body as subject matter or his own mind (as it exists up to that point) as subject matter. In the thought process it is always the mind functioning in the immediate present which is the initiating agent. The intellectual activity of the past has of course built up a complex of ideas, recallable through the memory mechanisms of the nervous system, that both conditions and aids present thinking. But the individual thinking *now* and deciding *now* is a free agent, and his past accumulation of knowledge is subject matter that he utilizes and adds to.

Basically the difference between agency and subject matter is that between *active* and *passive*. Only in his role as agent (active) does a man have freedom of choice; insofar as he is subject matter (passive), what happens to him is determined by the agents (active) that act upon him (passive).

Human beings, functioning as agent-causes, constitute the surging crest of an ongoing and unending movement of life, of an energetic and pulsating humanity. Just as important as what the environment makes of men is what men, in their role as agents, make of the environment. The environment challenges and men respond, fight back, overcome, advance to a higher level. Yet they do not always succeed in meeting the challenge. They may be defeated; they may succumb; they may also go far in ruining the environment, as when they lay waste immense areas of forest, pollute rivers, poison the air and exhaust the soil.

We now return to the theme of contingency. In an address at the Harvard Divinity School, William James remarked: "What is meant by saying that my choice of which way to walk home after the lecture is ambiguous and a matter of chance as far as the present moment is concerned? It means that both Divinity Avenue and Oxford Street are called; but that only one, and that one *either* one, shall be chosen." [126] Contingency is operative in the choice James is going to make because, first, it ensures that the two alternatives or potentialities confronting him are real and indeterminate in relation to his act of choosing.

Contingency is operative, second, because no deterministic law is impelling James to go home by one route or the other. He has built up no firm habit of walking home by one special street from the hall where he is lecturing. It cannot be emphasized too strongly that unless a human choice is part of a fixed if-then sequence, it is a free decision and also a contingent one. Contingency is operative, third, in the James choice because when he finally puts into effect his decision in favor, say, of Divinity Avenue, he initiates a chance concurrence between two separate and mutually independent event-streams or objects, namely, himself and the Avenue.

To analyze another instance of choice and chance, one evening at supper I decide that after the meal I shall go to a certain movie in my car, instead of taking a bus, a taxi or the subway. An hour or so later when I get into my sedan my volition is the immediate cause-stimulus for the event-stream that is myself intersecting with the event-stream represented by my automobile. When I turn the key to start the engine, I am bringing into play my own psycho-physical determinants, my "executive nerves," which thereby cause the mechanisms of the automobile to begin their deterministic functioning. Thus freedom, contingency and determinism coalesce in this familiar type of situation.

The example I have just given is a case of deciding to do something in advance and then doing it at the set time and place. This kind of decision enables me to change my mind before I make the final commitment of embodying the choice in action. But in many cases of free choice, perhaps the less important ones on the whole, the deciding and the acting are simultaneous. In driving my car to the movie theatre, I overtake a slow-moving auto. It is dark and I flash my bright lights to show the other driver that I want to pass him. My decision to pass and my flashing of the lights constitute a single unit of behavior in which *I decide to act by acting*.

Such behavior is typical of any activity requiring quick decision and prompt action. Take, for example, my two favorite sports of tennis and skiing. When I return a serve in tennis, I decide at the very moment of hitting the ball what stroke to use and where in the opposite court I shall try to place the ball. When skiing down a hill, I decide to turn and do turn simultaneously as I avoid ice, bumps and other skiers in weaving my way to the bottom of the slope.

Whether or not decision and execution immediately coalesce, the standard unit of free choice must include the resulting action, even when that action occurs some time after a man decides what he is going to do. Unless the action takes place almost simultaneously with the choice, we cannot be sure that it will be carried out as planned. Unforeseen circumstances may interfere, a person may change his mind, sudden death may intrude. Thus, a choice remains uncompleted, tentative, a mere intention—until it is *finalized* in the chosen action.

Contingency or chance frequently turns out to be disastrous for human beings in this precarious existence, particularly if they are caught off guard by Nature on the rampage as in a flood or hurricane. But in effectuating freedom of choice, men are able to take advantage of, to *exploit* the constant opportunities that contingency creates. These opportunities take the form of plural and protean potentialities. Both determinism and contingency can wreak havoc in human life; yet both can be tamed and put to excellent use by free choice combined with knowledge.

Dewey defines the situation: "In a world which was completely tight and exact in all its constituents, there would be no room for freedom. Contingency while it gives room does not fill that room. Freedom is an actuality when the recognition of relations, the stable element, is combined with the uncertain element, in the knowledge which makes foresight possible and secures intentional preparation for probable consequences. We are free in the degree in which we act knowing what we are about." [127]

It is often asserted that the free choice position implies causeless choices and actions. I trust my analysis has shown that this charge is unjustified. In terms of energy, causation resides in every decision, stimulating a man to make *a* choice, but not necessitating him to make *the* choice he does. For instance, a feeling of hunger is the proximate cause for my entering a restaurant in order to satisfy that want, but my hunger as cause does not impel me to select any particular dish among those listed upon the menu. Lamb chops, steak, chicken or bacon-and-eggs—each is a possibility and each adequate for gratifying my appetite. To generalize from this case, we can state that each of two or more alternative choices by a human being may be consistent with the initiating cause and a natural consequence of it.*

* Cf. F. C. S. Schiller, p. 120.

Professor Randall introduces a most important consideration: "Not all causes are exclusively 'push-of-energy' events, though all may well involve the expenditure of energy. In human life, many causes are foreseeings of the future consequences, natural structures understood. . . . Such foreseeings can enter in to impinge upon and modify other causal series; for causation being thus pluralistic, it is always possible in any particular case to add new determinations." [128]

Professor Hartshorne gives the basic background for my elementary example of choosing a good meal. "Every event," he writes, "has its cause or causes; so far we nearly all agree. . . . But not every event—indeed some of us would say, not *any* event in its concrete actuality—is fully and absolutely determined by its causes. In other words, an indeterminist . . . rejects a certain definition of 'cause,' namely that it is a condition, or set of conditions, from which only one outcome is possible, or from which, in principle or ideally, the outcome is wholly predictable.

"To be substituted for this is a definition which, whatever else it includes, involves the following requirement: the cause is a state of affairs such that when granted something more or less like what happens subsequently was 'bound to happen,' or (if you prefer) could safely have been predicted. Given dry TNT, a confined space, and a lighted fuse, there will inevitably, or with practically infinite probability, be an explosion; but it does not follow, and indeterminism denies, that the exact details of the explosion, the behavior of each atom and particle, will be the only possible ones (in principle, uniquely predictable) under the circumstances. . . .

"Our question, then, is whether causes or conditions determine happenings absolutely, or whether they merely limit more or less sharply what can happen. 'More or less sharply' will perhaps seem hopelessly vague. However, one may state the indeterminist or relativist view more subtly, as follows: events are always to an appropriate degree determined by their causal antecedents. And what is 'an appropriate degree'? I think we can give at least a rough answer to this question. A human being, in full possession of normal intelligence, surveying wide alternatives of action under general conceptions whose very meaning is that they admit highly divergent possible instances, must dispose of a wider range of possible reactions to a given situation than there is reason to attribute to a molecule reacting to its situation. . . . Inanimate nature involves the least scope of alternatives—and here the 'more or less determined' means 'more'; man involves the widest scope—and here it means very much 'less.' Thus we need not make man an arbitrary exception to the general principles of nature; he is but the intensive case of the general principles of creative action, of which causality is an aspect." [129]

Hartshorne's position that a certain looseness can be discerned in the causal joints of the cosmos is also that of Professor Čapek: "The present, though *co-determined* by the past, nevertheless contains an element of irreducible novelty. The individuality of a present event, or better, its *presentness* would be irremediably destroyed without this double feature of novelty and its dynamic cohesion with the anterior phases. . . . As far as the future is concerned, it is the *future* and not a disguised or hidden present as in the necessitarian scheme; it *will arise,* it is not *present.* But because it will not emerge 'ex nihilo,' but out of a particular present state, its *general direction* is outlined and thus it possesses some predictable features, the more predictable, the larger the statistical complexes of the elementary events considered." [130]

Continuing with this thought, Čapek says: ". . . we see why contingentism can be called a *relative determinism:* the future *is* determined, but only in its general character, never in its actual details. It is this general orientation of each present moment that contemporary physics grasps in the form of probabilistic laws." [131] *

The upshot of these various observations is that there is no uncaused cause which is initiated every time an individual exercises his power of choice. For a man's energies function as an unbroken continuum of cause and effect. What happens is that one component of those energies, the conscious self or agent, directs them into this channel or that in accordance with his reasoned choices. At the same time "The decider of a present issue is not simply identical with the self which resolved a previous issue, but is a new decider." [132] My new self of the immediate present only becomes completely determinate as I put into effect my chosen act. My choices, as they are actualized, function as both contingent causes and free causes. Yes, I—a thinking, dynamic, choosing agent—can be and frequently am *the free cause* of my own actions.

* Cf. pp. 50-51, 94.

The idea I am outlining here is sometimes known as *self-determination*. It was first clearly presented by the Greek philosopher Carneades, head of Plato's Academy at Athens in the second century B.C.; and was developed in some detail by Thomas Reid, Scottish philosopher of the eighteenth century and founder of the so-called Common Sense School. As I interpret self-determination, it means that when a man is acting as agent and not as passive subject matter for some other agent, he is the subjective source of his own behavior. Thus he is the free, present chooser and cause of his own actions. This theory holds that antecedent causes (the past) limit a person's behavior, but that the governing factor in any decision is the self exercising immediate causal initiative and functioning as a free agent always affected by the external world, yet not determined by it. As the late Professor Wm. Pepperell Montague of Columbia University puts it, we human beings possess the freedom ". . . at each present moment to modify and supplement our past by a spontaneous effort not predetermined by that past. . . ." [133]

Every free choice is by its very nature a contingent event, a one-shot agent-cause impinging upon other events. "Our decisions and intentions are initially unique in character. They refer to some context, state of affairs, or situation. We wish to deal with some action or thing. *Scientific propositions are general in character, but practical propositions are usually particular,* for they refer to an actual complex of affairs." [134] [Italics mine—C. L.]

An identifiable human choice made for the first time is never part of a deterministic pattern; it can become so only if it is repeated again and again in response to the self-same stimulus until a uniform relation comes to exist between them, and a new law is thereby established. A repeated choice that has grown into a settled habit could thus be said to be deterministically caused. In that case it becomes "second nature" and takes on or approaches the status of a conditioned reflex.*

Sociologists, economists, insurance companies and other authorities have been able in recent times to work out statistical studies that show with a high degree of probability how fairly large groups of Americans will react to this stimulus or that. However, no statistical chart even tries to predict what choices *specific individuals* within a group are going to make. It is safe to assert that the science of statistics does not weaken the case for freedom of choice.

During the week preceding May 30, 1966, experts in the automobile business, relying on statistics for previous years, predicted that between 460 and 540 individuals in the United States would die in auto accidents during the Memorial Day weekend. The number killed turned out to be 514. But no expert attempted to name in advance any one of the persons who would die in automobile crashes that weekend, and none of those persons expected that his life would suddenly be snuffed out as spring reached its zenith and all nature was in flower.

John Dewey confirms what I have been saying: "The present tendency among scientific men is to think of laws as statistical in nature—that is, as statements of an 'average' found in the behavior of an enormous number of

* Cf. pp. 44-45.

things, no two of which are exactly alike. If this line of thought be followed out, it implies that the existence of laws or uniformities and regularities among natural phenomena, human acts included, does not in the least exclude the item of choice as a distinctive fact having its own distinctive consequences. No law does away with individuality of existence, each having its own particular way of operating; for *a law is concerned with relations and hence presupposes the being and operation of individuals.* If choice is found to be a distinctive act, having distinctive consequences, then no appeal to the authority of scientific law can militate in any way against its reality." [135] [Italics mine—C. L.]

A basic error of the determinists is that they reduce everything to subject matter, ascribing to it all the powers of causation, that is, of bringing about change. But it is the agent-cause (Aristotle's *efficient cause*) alone that initiates change and constitutes the creative process. Theologians borrow this thesis when they describe their God as the First Cause; they never talk of a first *effect.* It is God as agent, as efficient cause, who has the power, the initiative and the freedom to be the First Cause and Creator.

We see this confusion concerning subject matter and agency again in the genetic fallacy that views men's actions solely in terms of their causal antecedents. This "container" theory of causation repeats the old mistake of supposing that there must be an inclusive similarity between a cause and its effect, so that all the properties of the effect somehow pre-exist in the cause. But each thing that exists is what it *does* rather than what it is caused by; its antecedents cannot negate its specific characteristics, activities and modes of interaction.

The lovely blossoming of a rose is just as real as the lowly roots from which it sprang. Water is caused by the interaction of hydrogen and oxygen. But water behaves in a way that could never be deduced from a study of hydrogen and oxygen separately; it would be absurd to claim that water cannot run downhill or satisfy a man's thirst because neither hydrogen nor oxygen does. With water there emerge new qualities and kinds of behavior quite dissimilar to those of its causal antecedents. Thus every phenomenon possesses a certain irreducible quality—namely, its individuality—that is at least as important a factor in its behavior as the prior causes that bring it into being or the external causes that later affect it.* In the words of Dr. Barrows Dunham: "Every event is genuinely new and has powers of its own. Accordingly, in the behavior of every entity there is always something that is not the effect of other causes." [136]

When the determinists eliminate Aristotle's efficient cause, which I have called the agent-cause, they also unwittingly eliminate time or process. In this way they deprive causation of its dynamic and successive quality. In other words, ". . . a completely necessitarian theory of causation makes time unreal by making the cause-and-effect relation *static* instead of a process of transition from a temporal antecedent to a temporal consequent." [137] [Italics mine—C. L.]

I remember Professor Woodbridge remarking in his

* Cf. pp. 85-86.

Columbia seminar on metaphysics that if there were no contingency, and determinism were true, everything would have happened already.* John Macmurray in his book *The Self as Agent* takes the same view: "The falsity of determinism lies simply in the dogma that the future is already determinate. But if this were so there would be no future; the future would be already past. . . . A determinate future is not a real future. The real future is the indeterminate which is determined in action, and in being determined becomes the past." [138] What both Woodbridge and Macmurray are saying is that universal determinism by implication abolishes time, so that time comes to a stop and there can be no future. Aristotle made a similar observation in the fourth century B. C.

   Returning for a moment to Laplace's suggestion that an omniscient mind could foresee the shape—and the content—of things to come for all future time, I think that what must be assumed here is that such a mind would be able to *deduce* all future events from all present events. Thus the necessity envisioned is the timeless necessity of logical deduction, and time is again dropped out of the picture. As Professor Čapek states, all forms of determinism commit "the fallacy of confusing causality with static relation." [139] In short, the determinists exclude the temporal push-of-energy element—the flow of continuity—from the cause-effect process; and fail to realize that the stimulus of agency, of efficient cause, is essential for the onward movement of man, life and Nature.

   * Cf. p. 101.

6
Some Practical Problems

I—Character and Freedom of Choice

An argument frequently advanced against the free choice thesis is that unless determinism be true, we cannot rely upon relatives, friends or public officials to act dependably in any serious situation or crisis. Only if their deeds flow deterministically from their established characters, the argument continues, can we be sure that they will make the right decisions and not be utterly capricious. Under this interpretation ethical conduct *demands* determinism, as does wisdom in the administration of government.

There are several answers to this line of thought. In the first place, a man of good character—intelligent, courageous, public-spirited—can put into effect a wide variety of possible actions, all of which are consistent with his goodness. This multiplicity of actions constitutes his "behavioral range." From what we know of this individual we can infer that he will in general act "in character" and so live up to his excellent record and reputation. That much can be predicted with considerable assurance. But the *specific* ways in which he will actualize his goodness are beyond the realm of predictability. It is in these concrete actualizations that his freedom of choice functions, at every point stemming from and based upon the person's fundamentally fine character.

Suppose a young lawyer who has shown intellectual calibre and moral idealism wishes to further to the best of his ability the movement to obtain full constitutional rights for the Negro people in the United States. Various opportunities exist for the extension of civil rights. He can become an attorney for the NAACP (National Association for the Advancement of Colored People); he can offer his services to CORE (Congress for Racial Equality); he can join the Lawyers Constitutional Defense Committee and commute to the deep South to defend civil rights workers illegally arrested; or he can bend his energies towards eliminating Negro ghettos and poverty pockets in some big northern city.

Whichever one of these alternatives the young man chooses, he will be doing a useful job for civil rights and expressing the high quality of his character. Yet from that quality it cannot be inferred or predicted which one of the alternatives he will select. His admirable character sets general—and desirable—limits within which his free choice will very probably operate, but it does not deterministically dictate the particular choices he will make within those extensive boundary lines. If we analyze the situation in terms of motives, similar conclusions follow. Human motives are usually quite general: One desires to obtain a good education, to marry an attractive woman, to be helpful to one's children, to do a good job in one's chosen work, to seek out recreation on the weekend, to serve one's country. Such motives have a broad sweep and do not predetermine the *precise* ways in which they will be actualized; "they incline without necessitating." *

William James offers another consideration: "A favorite argument against free-will is that if it be true, a man's murderer may as probably be his best friend as his worst enemy, a mother be as likely to strangle as to suckle her first-born, and all of us as ready to jump from fourth-story windows as to go out of front doors, etc. Users of this argument should properly be excluded from debate till they learn what the real question is. 'Free-will' does not say that everything that is physically conceivable is also morally possible. It merely says that of alternatives that really *tempt* our will more than one is really possible. Of course, the alternatives that do thus tempt our will are vastly fewer than the physical possibilities we can coldly fancy. . . ." [140]

In the second place, the determinist argument from stable character traits represents a static conception of human nature. Professor of Philosophy Wilfrid Sellars, of the University of Pittsburgh, points out: "To say of a person that his actions are predictable is not always a compliment. Even a person who can be counted on to do what is right is marked down a little when it is said that one can predict

---

* My reasoning on pages 139-41 illustrates again that universals or general ideas in a man's mind do not imply which particulars under them are to be actualized.

exactly what he will do. For to say this implies that he meets situations in routine ways, never thinking things through afresh or gaining new insight. . . . To be a rational being is to be a being who is capable of action that is not in character, and hence cannot be predicted within the framework of the manifest image." [141]

The intelligent and high-principled individual is never wholly satisfied with what he is and what he has accomplished; he is continually striving to improve. Actions not only express character; they also build it, as they reinforce or add to those habit patterns that are the foundation of virtue. "The essence of ethical reform, and of mere growth even, involves precisely a distinction between the present self as *the* self, and the past as an erstwhile friend now become like a distant acquaintance, an awkward relative or even an enemy." [142] Time and again, mediocre, self-seeking or corrupt individuals have been moved by some compelling experience, as St. Paul on the road to Damascus, to reform their lives to a far-reaching degree, to become "twice-born men." Others, who have demonstrated courage and integrity in the past, may start to falter, to compromise, to retreat.

Significant new beginnings, for the better or for the worse, occur in the life of every human being; and it is freedom of choice that makes this possible. Indeed, every freely conceived choice, with its appropriate action, constitutes to a certain extent a new beginning within the space-time continuum, a new point of departure that may set in motion an entire series of deterministic sequences.

Insofar as morality in general is concerned, Dewey gives us the gist of the matter: "No individual or group will be judged by whether they come up to or fall short of some fixed result, but by the direction in which they are moving. The bad man is the man who no matter how good he *has* been is beginning to deteriorate, to grow less good. The good man is the man who no matter how morally unworthy he *has* been is moving to become better." [143]

In the third place, those who claim that determinism is inherent in the functioning of a firmly established character neglect the fact that this character did not spring full-blown from the womb, but took many years to develop—from infancy to childhood to youth to maturity. And that development into a hard-boiled gangster or into a crusading idealist was in good measure the result of a thousand and one free choices which gradually molded the settled character of full maturity. If a person has freedom of choice in his early life, it is not logical to deny his possession of that capability in his later years.

In the fourth place, the proposition that a person can be relied upon only if his choices are deterministically governed locates causal efficacy entirely in the past and robs the present of its predominant role. It is the old confusion between subject matter and agency.* Using a somewhat different terminology, Warden Austin Farrer of Keble College, Oxford, makes this same point. He considers it vital to distinguish beween *antecedent* interest, which inclines us to a certain line of action, and "the *concomitant*

* Cf. pp. 125-26.

interest we take in developing that line of action." Both these types of interest play an essential part in freely chosen action.

Warden Farrer says: "Antecedent interest, springing out of disposition, must first arise, or . . . the agent will simply not be there, or on the job. If, when he proceeded to the job, the antecedent interest remained the whole motive of his action, he would be controlled by the dead hand of his own past. The past nothing can alter— not even the gods can do it, says the Greek proverb; a choice determined by antecedent interest would be determined indeed. But a little attention to life as it is lived will suffice to lay the spectre of necessity. Out of antecedent interest is born an interest concomitant with the action it motives: an interest inseparable from the action itself, and equally flexible. . . . Every voluntary transition we make from one phase of action to another has antecedent interest behind it, and concomitant interest dwelling upon it." [144]

Indubitably, the innate physical and mental qualities with which a man is born are of decisive import in shaping his character and career. Those qualities arise through the multitudinous genes that are transmitted through the germ cells of each parent. Except in the rare cases of identical twins, no two male-female combinations of genes are the same. During a single act of procreation any one of the 300 to 500 million spermatozoa of the father may unite with the ovum of the mother. Each such possible union must result in a different combination of genes and in a different individual.

A man is not able to choose either his parents or his

genes; his genetic inheritance is obviously beyond his control. From his standpoint, it is a plain matter of good luck or bad luck. A person physically crippled or deformed from birth is handicapped from the start. And we cannot expect a normal or wise exercise of free choice by those who are born Mongolian idiots or are congenitally feebleminded in some other way. However, in the large, all but a handful of human beings are normal at birth, with normal capabilities and potentialities. Their inherent qualities, however varying from one man to another, can be described only in the most general terms. They cannot and do not determine the individual's every choice and act, although they do establish limits, and very wide ones, to the possibilities open to him.*

II—*Forbearance and Ethics*

Freedom of choice means that a man is both free to do something and free *not* to do it. I am free to march in a civil rights demonstration and I am free not to. I am free to buy an evening newspaper and I am free not to. Thus an individual can refrain or forbear when the possibility of some action arises. In such case his stance may be simply forbearance in the form of inaction. When a man refuses a second martini, it may be that he will not take a glass of

---

* An apt simile from card games is: Your inborn qualities and characteristics are the hand you are dealt; your freedom of choice is the way you play it.

tomato juice instead, but will abstain from any drink at all.

If free choice exists, a person can look back on any decision and correctly say, "I could have chosen and done otherwise." The determinist, on the other hand, insists that such a thought is pure illusion and that a person at all times is absolutely necessitated to do precisely what he does do. According to the determinist's logic, he could not have done otherwise, either in the sense of doing something different or of forbearing altogether.*

This situation makes possible an analysis that I believe is most significant for the question of freedom of choice. Professor Arthur Danto of Columbia University has outlined the argument in a subtly reasoned essay, "Freedom and Forbearance." [145]

Professor Danto follows through with the implications involved when a man possesses the power both to do an action *a* and to refrain from doing it. He writes: "We are asking now whether *m* could be under conditions such that he could not do other than forbear doing *a* and still have full power with regard to *a*. We are asking whether, under those conditions, *m* is unable to do *a*, while yet forbearing from doing *a*, and still not in the situation of having only partial control. I would like to say that these conditions cannot jointly hold, that forbearance under the condition of full power with regard to *a* is incompatible with that forbearance being determined.

"For if I am determined to forbear, and cannot do otherwise, then, in just the sense in which the determinist requires, I am unable to do *a*. But it seems perfectly plain that, when a man is unable to do *a*, his not doing *a* is never a matter of his forbearance. Robinson Crusoe may have been capable of fathering thousands, but a necessary condition was lacking in his island home for him to exercise that power. So we do not and cannot say that he then forbore from fathering children. . . .

"If there are forbearances, determinism is wrong. It says that we cannot do other than what we in fact do, and if we are unable to do other than what we in fact do, we cannot forbear. . . . That there are forbearances, I think, each of us knows well enough. Unless we are incontinent, we forbear frequently, and our language testifies to this recognized fact." [146]

Attempting to interpret Professor Danto, and enlarging upon him a bit, I arrive at the following: To be consistent, the determinist must hold that if a man is necessitated to forbear from doing *a*, he is and was unable to do *a*. But this runs counter to the normal situation in which a man possesses the simultaneous power either to do *a* or not to do it. Of course, if an individual has been hypnotized to carry out *a*, then his ordinary freedom is in abeyance and he will not have the capacity to refrain from doing it. If in fact, however, a person is unable to do *a*, it is because some essential condition, either internal or external, is wanting for his doing *a*. This is the real meaning of inability to do something.

Robinson Crusoe was unable to beget children because there were no females of the species on his island. Hence it would not make sense to claim that he forbore from begetting children. However, the situation would have been very different had Crusoe rescued from the cannibals not only Friday, but also his attractive young sister, Fridianna. Then Crusoe might truly have forborne from the act of procreation, despite great temptation, because the lovely Fridianna was a heathen or because there was no official on hand who could legally marry them. This would have been real—indeed heroic—forbearance on the part of Crusoe. But if this sexual restraint had been determined in advance, it would have been a wholly necessitated non-action and no forbearance at all.

All of this adds up to the generalization that if, as the determinists assert, men can never act otherwise than they do or don't, then clearly they cannot forbear from doing *anything. For in order to forbear, one must at the same time be able both to do the thing and refrain from doing it.* Under the sway of determinism the not-doing would always be automatic, with no possibility present for the doing. My refraining from a second martini at a cocktail party amounts to meaningful forbearance only if to begin with I was able to choose the second martini. If I was unable all along to accept the second martini, as the determinist must say, then what would I be forbearing from when I declined it? Forbearance would be an impossibility if fate had already ruled out my choice of a second drink, just as forbearance would be an impossibility if the supply of martinis had run out.

The final result is that words such as *forbearance, self-restraint, refraining* and *abstaining* have no significant meaning in the language of determinism. The determinist might reply: "All right, there is no such thing as forbearance! So what?" This is not a good answer, since no philosophy can be sound or convincing if it denies the reality of everyday human experience.

In the realm of ethics nothing is more significant than forbearance; it is the main import of all virtues that are expressed in negative language. Eight of the Ten Commandments are in this form, such as: "Thou shalt not steal," "Thou shalt not kill," "Thou shalt not bear false witness against thy neighbor." Human virtues can of course be expressed in a positive form, but generally accepted principles and ideals of ethical conduct would have to be revised almost beyond recognition if true forbearance were impossible, as the determinist position implies.

Thus the determinist dispensation plays havoc with traditional concepts not only of regret and forbearance, but also of praise and blame, altruism and selfishness, bravery and cowardice, even of good and bad. Determinism makes such distinctions as inappropriate as the attribution of ethical responsibility to a shooting star, a thunderstorm or a lilac bush. What can virtue mean when there are no intelligible grounds for discriminating between a so-called good act and a so-called bad act, since both are equally predestinate, both the consequence of inexorable causation operating before a man is born? How can there be moral responsibility for the individual when all his choices and his entire course of conduct are preordained by the Spinner of the Years, the Turner of the Wheel, the decrees of Fate, the march of history or the forces of economics?

To praise and to blame are natural proclivities of human beings, useful for the inculcation of ethical standards and to the democratic process in public affairs. But determinism turns judgments of praise into sentimental delusions and judgments of blame into unreasonable derogations of character. True enough, such judgments are often mistaken, but it does not follow that they are never justified or that they refer to nothing real in human conduct.

Speaking of social determinism, Sir Isaiah Berlin states that ". . . it may, indeed, be a true doctrine. But if it is true, and if we begin to take it seriously, then, indeed, the changes in our language, our moral notions, our attitudes toward one another, our views of history, of society and of everything else will be too profound to be even adumbrated. . . . If social and psychological determinism were established as an accepted truth, our world would be transformed far more radically than was the teleological world of the classical and middle ages by the triumphs of mechanistic principles or those of natural selection. Our words—our modes of speech and thought—would be transformed in literally unimaginable ways; the notions of choice, of voluntary action, of responsibility, freedom, are so deeply imbedded in our outlook, that our new life, as creatures in a world genuinely lacking these concepts, can, I should maintain, literally not be conceived by us. . . . As for the attempt to 'reinterpret' these notions so as to bring them into conformity with determinism, this can be achieved only at the cost of altering their meanings beyond applicability to our normal experience." [147]

I am not suggesting, by my quotations from Berlin, that Nature necessarily conforms to our linguistic usages. Yet the built-in language habits of Homo sapiens as regards choice, freedom and morality—habits that have evolved over aeons of time—are at least some indication of the psychological patterns that develop most naturally in human beings. Those patterns point toward, without by any means establishing, the existence of freedom of choice.

III—Regret, Crime and Insanity

While free choice is usually associated with ethical behavior, Professor Demos rightly states that "freedom is not revealed in *moral* experience alone, but is in fact prior to it. A man may conceivably have no sense of right or wrong; he may be deciding what to do in complete oblivion of what he ought to do. He may nevertheless be aware while so deciding that he is free, for the decision to recognize moral standards or the decision to discard or ignore them is itself a free choice." [148]

Furthermore, men frequently make rather unimportant choices in which no real question of ethical conduct arises. A moral issue is involved only when from a *social* viewpoint one alternative is better than another, is more conducive to the welfare of the group and is therefore to be judged good or bad, better or worse. In this type of situation an individual may realize, quickly or after considerable deliberation, what he *ought* to do, but may decide to do something else because of some insistent personal desire or temptation.

Here the *I ought* implies the freedom of *I can, but need not*, a point much stressed by Immanuel Kant. St. Paul gives a classic formulation of what only too often happens: "The good that I would I do not: but the evil which I would not, that I do." [149] If an individual later looks back upon some action and finds it repugnant, he is likely to reflect, "I could have chosen and done differently, but did not." This is why remorse can be so poignant and the pangs of conscience so acute.

There has been a continuing debate over the precise meaning of "I could have done otherwise." Determinists Moritz Schlick and Professor Patrick Nowell-Smith, of the University of Kent, are typical of those who contend that the locution merely means that I could have acted otherwise if I had so chosen, but that then I would have been a differently constituted person. This interpretation seems to amount to a truism: "If I *had* chosen differently, then I *could* have chosen differently." However, true freedom of choice implies that I, possessing the self-same character and intellect, could have acted otherwise *because* (not *if*) I had the power to choose otherwise under the identical circumstances at the time of the choice. In short, supposing that I was confronted with three genuine alternatives, I was free to select any one of them up till the very moment I made a final decision.

In general, those who believe in free choice hold that a man does not have moral responsibility for his choices and acts, unless he could have chosen and have acted otherwise in the way I have just described. Professors Schlick and Nowell-Smith, on the other hand, think that a man is morally responsible "only to the degree that rewards and punishments can alter his future conduct. It makes no difference in their view whether the individual could have chosen to act otherwise *at the time.* The critical point is whether he can, *in the future,* be *made* to act otherwise or even to choose otherwise. If so, then he should be held responsible for his present action, i.e., he should be subject to praise or blame, reward or punishment." [150]

In his essay "Is 'Free Will' a Pseudo-Problem?" Charles A. Campbell, Professor Emeritus at the University of Glasgow, makes a good point in answering Professor Schlick: "We do not ordinarily consider the lower animals to be morally responsible. But *ought* we not to do so if Schlick is right about what we mean by moral responsibility? It is quite possible, by punishing the dog who absconds with the succulent chops designed for its master's luncheon, favorably to influence its motives in respect of its future behavior in like circumstances. If moral responsibility is to be linked with punishment as Schlick links it, and punishment conceived as a form of education, we should surely hold the dog morally responsible. The plain fact, of course, is that we don't. We don't, because we suppose that the dog 'couldn't help it': that its action (unlike what we usually believe to be true of human beings) was simply a link in a continuous chain of causes and effects. . . ." [151]

As William James points out, the determinist thesis makes mishmash out of feelings of regret. Yet, as he states, "Hardly an hour passes in which we do not wish that some-

thing might be otherwise; and happy indeed are those of us
whose hearts have never echoed the wish of Omar Khayyám

> That we might clasp, ere closed, the book of fate,
> And make the writer on a fairer leaf
> Inscribe our names, or quite obliterate." [152]

James goes on to say: "When murders and treacheries
cease to be sins, regrets are theoretic absurdities and errors.
. . . And what sense can there be in condemning ourselves
for taking the wrong way, unless we need have done nothing
of the sort, unless the right way was open to us as well? I
cannot understand the willingness to act, no matter how we
feel, without the belief that acts are really good and bad. I
cannot understand the belief that an act is bad, without regret at its happening. I cannot understand regret without the
admission of real, genuine possibilities in the world. Only
then is it other than a mockery to feel, after we have failed
to do our best, that an irreparable opportunity is gone
from the universe, the loss of which it must forever after
mourn." [153]

Taking a gruesome wife-killing as his case in point,
James shows that determinism implies a pessimistic view
of the world: "The judgment of regret calls the murder bad.
Calling a thing bad means, if it means anything at all, that
the thing ought not to be, that something else ought to be in
its stead. Determinism, in denying that anything else can be
in its stead, virtually defines the universe as a place in which
what ought to be is impossible,—in other words, as an or-

ganism whose constitution is afflicted with an incurable taint, an irremediable flaw." [154] *

In the field of criminal law Clarence Darrow (1857-1938), renowned American attorney, successfully utilized the philosophy of determinism in which he sincerely believed. Repeatedly he defended men charged with murder or robbery in the courts on the grounds that since their every thought and action was predetermined, they could not rightly be held morally accountable for their crimes. By this argument he not infrequently obtained acquittals, or sentences less severe than were to be expected.

In his final plea to the court in the famous murder case of Nathan Leopold and Richard Loeb in 1924, Darrow read in full a poem, "The Culprit," by a noted determinist, A. E. Housman. In it a young man soliloquizes on the eve of his hanging:

> The night my father got me
>   His mind was not on me;
> He did not plague his fancy
>   To muse if I should be
>   The son you see.
>
> The day my mother bore me
>   She was a fool and glad,
> For all the pain I cost her,
>   That she had borne the lad
>   That borne she had.
>
> My mother and my father
>   Out of the light they lie;

* Cf. Thomas Hardy, p. 27.

155

The warrant could not find them,
    And here 'tis only I
    Shall hang so high.

Oh let not man remember
    The soul that God forgot,
But fetch the county kerchief
    And noose me in the knot,
    And I will rot.

For so the game is ended
    That should not have begun.
My father and my mother
    They had a likely son,
    And I have none.[155]

After reciting Housman's poem, Darrow declared: "No one knows what will be the fate of the child he gets or the child she bears; the fate of the child is the last thing they consider. This weary old world goes on, begetting, with birth and with living and with death; and all of it is blind from the beginning to the end. I do not know what it was that made these boys do this mad act, but I do know there is a reason for it. I know they did not beget themselves. I know that any one of an infinite number of causes reaching back to the beginning might be working out in these boys' minds, whom you are asked to hang in malice and in hatred and injustice, because someone in the past has sinned against them." [156] *

In 1966 Judge David I. Bazelon of the United States

* Loeb was killed in 1936 by a prison inmate; Leopold was paroled in 1958 and unconditionally freed in 1963.

Court of Appeals in Washington, D. C., stated in an address before the New York Civil Liberties Union: "From my sixteen years' experience on the bench, I would say that almost all the perpetrators [of street crimes of violence] come from the bottom of the socio-economic cultural barrel —from among the ignorant, the unemployed and often unemployable. Because they are often deprived of what we call a moral upbringing, our code has little meaning for them. And they have little incentive to observe it since they are virtually excluded from the advantages of our economic and political life. Crime is just one of a cluster of social ills—family breakdowns, mental disorders, unsupervised youths, school dropouts, alcoholism, and drug addiction— which beset this group." [157]

I accept Judge Bazelon's analysis of the situation, but must point out that only a small minority of the underprivileged group commit crime and that many members of that group in American cities rise above their environment to become successful and respected citizens. It is my claim that they do this by exercising their freedom of choice, though obviously that freedom is drastically curtailed and circumscribed for the millions of Americans who continue to live in urban slums and poverty pockets. Freedom of choice, however, is *always* subject to some limitation; but as I noted earlier, no matter how drastic the limitation may be, it cannot totally nullify the innate and original freedom of the individual.

Another consideration relevant here is that in modern society a large proportion of criminals come from middle-class or upper-class homes where living standards are comparatively high and educational opportunities plentiful. Obvious examples are the two young murderers, Leopold and Loeb, who grew up in well-to-do families, never knew any kind of economic pressure and enjoyed boundless cultural advantages. Class origins cannot account for the enormous incidence of graft in American political life for the past hundred years or more. The truth is that all criminals and grafters, whether they grew up in a good environment or bad, have misused their freedom of choice, usually with a get-rich-quick motive, to follow an iniquitous and lawless course of conduct.

A humane and high-minded friend of mine, who has been a social worker in a slum district, told me about a young tough in the area who had been convicted of robbery. "Why," my friend said, "you *have* to be a determinist when you are in this sort of work. If I had been brought up like young Jones, I would certainly have become a robber, too." This statement I consider to be distressing nonsense. It represents the same attitude as that of Clarence Darrow and can be described as *sentimental determinism* motivated by sincere, if exaggerated, sympathy for the underdogs in society.

The laws of the United States make provision for the so-called "irresistible impulse" test. This takes into account that an individual may be unable to keep himself from committing a crime, even though he knows it to be legally and morally wrong. In this class of crimes is kleptomania: the persistent, neurotic predisposition to steal, though no motive of economic need or advantage may be present. Chronic alcoholics are irresistibly impelled. And confirmed drug addicts have such an overwhelming desire to continue their habit that they will murder or rob to obtain money for the purchase of heroin or marijuana.

In Anglo-American law, if a defendant is deemed insane and therefore not responsible for the criminal choices he has made, he may be excused from standing trial or acquitted if his trial takes place. For more than a century criminal law in England and the United States has followed the M'Naughton Rule of 1843. This rule takes its name from Daniel M'Naughton, a paranoiac who suffered from a persecution complex and thought that Britain's Tory Prime Minister, Sir Robert Peel, was his chief persecutor. He went to London planning to assassinate Peel as the Tory leader drove by in his carriage. However, on the fatal day the Prime Minister decided to ride in Queen Victoria's coach because she was absent from the city, while his private secretary, Edward Drummond, rode in Peel's carriage. With astonishing ease, M'Naughton shot and killed Drummond.

At his trial the assassin was found not guilty because of impressive medical evidence that he was insane. After his acquittal, M'Naughton was sent to an insane asylum for the rest of his life. In its decision in March 1843 the court declared that "to establish a defense on the ground of insanity, it must be clearly proved that, at the time of the committing of the act, the party accused was laboring under such a defect of reason, from disease of the mind, as not to know the nature and quality of the act he was doing, or, if he did know it, that he did not know he was doing what was wrong." [158]

During the past few decades judges, lawyers and criminologists have become increasingly dissatisfied with the M'Naughton Rule as a guideline for determining mental competence. In 1966 a United States Court of Appeals in New York City adopted a new test in the case of Charles Freeman, a peddler of heroin. The court stated: "A person is not responsible for criminal conduct if at the time of such conduct as a result of mental disease or defect he lacks substantial capacity either to appreciate the wrongfulness of his conduct or to conform his conduct to the requirements of law." [159] This rule, the court added, ". . . reflects awareness that from the perspective of psychiatry absolutes are ephemeral and gradations inevitable. By employing the telling word 'substantial' to modify 'incapacity,' the rule emphasizes that 'any' incapacity is not sufficient to justify avoidance of criminal responsibility but that 'total' incapacity is also unnecessary." [160]

Madmen who become criminals lack the power of free choice, especially in an ethical sense, with respect to those aspects of life in which their mental disease expresses itself. But they may be very cunning and resourceful in working out the details of a crime. And lunatics in general may have lucid intervals. The insane, criminal or otherwise, do retain some measure of freedom of choice.

Legal rules about the criminally insane such as I have been citing are particularly helpful in borderline cases, but many crimes are committed in which the coroner, sheriff or district attorney is able without much difficulty to identify the guilty party as mentally ill. The following tragic story from *The New York Times* of May 28, 1966, illustrates this point:

"Warren, Ohio, May 27 (UPI)—A schizophrenic steelworker, whose mental disturbances kept him chronically out of work, went berserk early today and killed his wife, four children and himself. Michael Collins, a 31 year-old mental patient diagnosed as a 'paranoid schizophrenic,' fired 23 shots in his small frame home on the outskirts of town. Fourteen of them hit his family, killing his wife, Minnie, 28, and the children, David, 7; Andy, 6; Silas, 4, and Viola, 3. Coroner Joseph Sudimak said Collins stabbed and clubbed his wife before shooting her, then shot his children, set a fire in the attic and turned the rapid-firing .22-caliber bolt-action rifle on himself."

However, by far the greater proportion of criminals in the modern world are not mentally ill. And the extent of crime in the U.S.A. and other nations cogently illustrates the terrible misuse of freedom of choice. In the United States in 1964 there were 9,250 murders, with an average of one every hour; while during the same year more than 184,000 physical assaults with intent to kill or commit serious injury took place. Crimes of violence are very often crimes of passion in which a man gives way to anger, jealousy or some other strong emotion.

My discussion of crime is most pertinent because it throws the spotlight of implication on the determinist thesis. I earlier cited the "irresistible impulse" test in criminal law.

"On the determinist theory of action, *every* impulse from which a man does in fact act is irresistible." [161] [Italics mine—C. L.] This inference holds whether his act is good or bad. Suppose an individual has an impulse to do each of three things, *a*, *b*, and *c*, and that he is about to make a choice among them. Under the determinist dispensation, when he chooses and acts on *b*, the fulfilment of his impulse to do *b* was predetermined; it was therefore irresistible.

In the dialectic of determinism, then, not only the criminally insane but the ethically good are moved by irresistible impulse. Thus a man of affectionate disposition has an irresistible impulse to be kind to his children and his mother-in-law; a public-spirited citizen has an irresistible impulse to expose the graft at City Hall; George Washington had an irresistible impulse to tell the truth after he cut down the cherry tree.

A variation on the "irresistible impulse" theme is to look at human choice from the viewpoint of hypnosis. If a man is hypnotized to perform a certain action, he then has an "irresistible impulse" to do it and has temporarily lost his freedom of choice. Exploring this thought further, we may say that determinism implies that all men at all times choose and act according to the irresistible impulses generated by the great cosmic hypnotist, Fate.

What all this makes plain is that the determinist philosophy, when forced to face up to its full implications, can offer no justification for making moral judgments. It must treat with generous ethical impartiality hardened criminals and persons who have a long record of altruistic service to their fellow men. Thus, all thieves are really kleptomaniacs, born with an overpowering tendency to steal; and confessed murderers should be sent to the psychiatrist's couch and a rest home in the country rather than to jail.

IV—Walden Two

In his popular novel *Walden Two*, Dr. B. F. Skinner, Professor of Psychology at Harvard University, gives a fascinating account of a small-scale American Utopia in which psychology and the other behavioral sciences are benevolently used to control completely the lives of every member of the community from birth to death. Basic in Professor Skinner's portrayal of his ideal society is a thorough-going determinism and an explicit denial that human beings have freedom of choice.

The hero of *Walden Two*, T. E. Frazier, who has studied at graduate school, outlines the methods and aims of the new Walden: "Well, what do you say to the design of personalities? Would that interest you? The control of temperament? Give me the specifications, and I'll give you the man! What do you say to the control of motivation, building the interests which will make men most productive and most successful? Does that seem to you fantastic? Yet some of the techniques are available, and more can be worked out experimentally. Think of the possibilities! A society in which there is no failure, no boredom, no duplication of effort! . . . Let us control the lives of our children and see what we can make of them. . . .[162]

"Now that we *know* how positive reinforcement works, and why negative doesn't, we can be more deliberate and hence more successful, in our cultural design. We can achieve a sort of control under which the controlled, though they are following a code much more scrupulously than·was ever the case under the old system, nevertheless *feel free*. They are doing what they want to do, not what they are forced to do. That's the source of the tremendous power of positive reinforcement—there's no restraint and no revolt. By a careful cultural design, we control not the final behavior, but the *inclination* to behave—the motives, the desires, the wishes. The curious thing is that in that case *the question of freedom never arises*." [163]

As to free choice, Frazier says flatly: "I deny that freedom exists at all. I must deny it—or my program would be absurd. You can't have a science about a subject matter which hops capriciously about. Perhaps we can never *prove* that man isn't free; it's an assumption. But the increasing success of a science of behavior makes it more and more plausible." [164]

Speaking for himself directly, Professor Skinner comments in the same vein: "The hypothesis that man is not free is essential to the application of scientific method to the study of human behavior. The free inner man who is held responsible for the behavior of the external biological organism is only a prescientific substitute for the kinds of causes which are discovered in the course of a scientific analysis. All these alternative causes lie *outside* the individual." [165] Skinner's approach is reminiscent of the behaviorist psychology propounded by Dr. John B. Watson in his well-known book, *Psychology, from the Standpoint of a Behaviorist* (1919).

It seems to me that *Walden Two* goes far beyond the very general socio-economic planning recommended by many intelligent observers of the current scene to suggest a community whose underlying motif is the inculcation of the conditioned reflex in all phases of life, a complete scientific brain-washing for the purpose of producing the good society. In George Orwell's *1984*, brain-washing is utilized for the creation of an abhorrent society in which an absolute dictator, "Big Brother," wields unrestrained power for evil ends. However, political brain-washing goes on to some degree in all countries in which the government and its supporters control and manipulate the main means of communication, such as the newspapers, radio, TV and book publishing. The fact is that brain-washing is merely indoctrination or advertising or propaganda escalated to the nth degree. It is nothing new in history.

In his book *On Becoming a Person*, Professor Rogers goes far in refuting Skinner's views. Rogers objects to the sort of world "which Skinner explicitly (and many other scientists implicitly) expect and hope for in the future. To me this kind of world would destroy the human person as I have come to know him in the deepest moments of psychotherapy. In such moments I am in relationship with a person who is spontaneous, who is responsibly free, that is, aware of this freedom to choose who he will be, and aware also of the consequences of his choice. To believe, as Skinner holds, that all this is an illusion, and that spontaneity, freedom, responsibility, and choice have no real existence, would be impossible for me." [166]

Rogers shows that Skinner runs into serious self-contradiction when he decides that the inhabitants of his projected Utopia are to be informed, skillful, well-behaved and productive. For this is a personal and subjective choice on his part. "He might have chosen to make men submissive, dependent, and gregarious, for example. Yet by his own statement in another context man's 'capacity to choose,' his freedom to select his course and to initiate action—these powers do not exist in the scientific picture of man." [167]

Generalizing from Rogers' analysis, we see that in a dictatorship, whether benevolent or malevolent, the one-man ruler or the Executive Council that runs the country is required constantly to make important choices. Unless we postulate a supernatural, all-determining Deity, there is nobody above the dictator and the Executive Council to give orders. There is nobody, if I may coin a word, to *determinize* the determiners. We must conclude that if freedom of choice is ruled out at the bottom of a socio-political system, it has to be given a place at the top.*

The Skinner-Rogers controversy brings to mind the claim that psychiatry and psychoanalysis strengthen the case for determinism by indicating that unconscious desires, motives, complexes or aberrations can govern in strict

---

* Similarly, there must be a human being who decides on which problems are to be fed into the mechanical nerve cells of the automatic computer, the "electric brain" of cybernetics.

cause-effect fashion a man's conscious reasoning and choices. Such "reasoning" then becomes a mere rationalization of deep-seated and hidden psychological states or neuroses that originated in early childhood.

Referring to these subconscious forces that control the conscious personality, Professor John Hospers of Brooklyn College offers an apt analogy: "The man himself does not know what the inner clockwork is; he is like the hands on the clock, thinking they move freely over the face of the clock." [168] And Professor Hospers goes so far as to say: "To be sure, the domination by the unconscious in the case of 'normal' individuals is somewhat more benevolent than the tyranny and despotism exercised in neurotic cases, and therefore the former have evoked less comment; but the principle remains in all cases the same: the unconscious is the master of every fate and the captain of every soul." [169]

I cannot accept this extreme position. Subconscious stimuli play a part in everyone's life, but I deny that they dominate human behavior except in the case of relatively few abnormal individuals. Free choice remains the normal possession of normal persons throughout the world. What the psychological sciences do establish beyond doubt is that there are exceptions to the operation of freedom of choice; that this freedom is canceled out, diminished or interfered with by the compulsive or otherwise abnormal patterns typical of neurotic, psychopathic or psychotic personalities.

If freedom of choice exists, certain psychoanalysts and psychiatrists who depend on Freudian concepts will need to revise their ideology considerably. For instance, the Freudian notion of a universal Oedipus complex among human beings withers away to a large extent when free choice is taken seriously. It will then be seen that a son may come to disagree with his father on political, economic or other issues, not primarily because he has an Oedipean father-hostility, but because of rational choices made after careful reflection. In my judgment an impressive proportion, if not a majority, of sons have a good, affectionate relationship with their fathers and do not develop psychological states such as the so-called Oedipus complex.

The lengths to which Freudian analysis is sometimes carried are typified in the book *Thomas Woodrow Wilson, Twenty-eighth President of the United States: A Psychological Study* (1967), by Sigmund Freud * and William C. Bullitt. The authors admit that President Wilson in his youth had an excellent relation with his father, whom he greatly admired. Hence Freud and Bullitt argue that Wilson's normal Oedipus complex was suppressed and had to find an outlet in various "surrogates" whom Wilson hated, such as Senator Henry Cabot Lodge and the French statesman, Raymond Poincaré. But Wilson's reasoned conclusions as to the League of Nations and international relations in general gave him ample grounds for bitter feelings towards his political enemy, Lodge, and Poincaré. So it is patently absurd to claim that Wilson's foreign policies, and personal attitudes resulting therefrom, were deterministically caused by his non-existent father-hostility.

* Since Dr. Freud actually wrote only the Foreword to this book, there is justified doubt as to how much he agreed with the volume as a whole.

7
Summary and Conclusion

In this book I have presented what to me are the most telling arguments for the objective existence of freedom of choice and the non-existence of universal, all-governing determinism. Ten main points stand out:

First, there is the strong, immediate, common-sense intuition in practically all human beings that we possess true freedom when choosing between real alternatives; and that retrospectively we are entitled to say, "I could have chosen otherwise." The theory of determinism is out of joint with the everyday experience of mankind. Admittedly, many a doctrine initially supported by common sense, such as the belief that the earth is flat, has been disproved by scientific investigation. But neither science nor logic nor any other intellectual discipline has disproved freedom of choice; on the contrary, the common-sense view here is reinforced by important data from science and by potent reasoning from philosophy.

Second, since human choice is always limited and conditioned by the past and by present circumstances, there can be no such thing as *absolute* freedom of choice. But there can be and is *relative* free choice co-existing with relative determinism. Determinism in the form of if-then causal sequences governs much of the human body's functioning and much of external Nature. Man utilizes free choice to further his well-being by taking advantage of established scientific laws and machines embodying determinism.

Third, the existence of chance or contingency as an ultimate trait of Nature negates the thesis of a total and exclusive determinism or necessity operating throughout the cosmos and human life. Contingency is readily seen in the unique intersection of mutually independent event-streams between which there was previously no causal connection. All natural laws take the form of if-then sequences or relations. The *if* factor is obviously conditional and demonstrates the continual co-existence of contingency with necessity. In fact, contingency and necessity are correlatives, and both rank as metaphysical ultimates. Furthermore, scientific theories of probability imply the existence of contingency.

Fourth, potentiality is another cosmic ultimate that undermines the determinist position. Potentiality looks toward the future and means that every object and event in the universe possesses *plural* possibilities of behavior, interaction and development. For the determinist, however, multiple potentialities are an illusion, since his theory demands that in every case only one potentiality is possible, namely, the potentiality of what actually happens. Such an interpretation strips potentiality of its fundamental meaning. When we relate the causal pattern to potentiality, we find that causation as mediated through free choice can have its appropriate effect in the actualization of any one of a number of relevant possibilities. In my next point I give a concrete example of the way this happens.

Fifth, the normal processes of human thought tend to show that freedom of choice is real. Thinking constantly goes on in terms of general conceptions or universals under which a number of varying particulars can be subsumed. An individual who has the general idea of "vacation travel" is likely to consider several places to which he may go. These different places constitute genuine alternatives or potentialities from which he can freely choose. Thus, a man who is deliberating in order to solve a problem relies upon both universals and potentiality, both of which point towards free choice.

Sixth, the fact that only the present exists and that it is always some present activity or force which produces the past, controverts the determinist claim that antecedent causes determine both present and future. In the determinist philosophy, time loses its dynamic character, becomes spatialized and is absorbed into a timeless All. In the freedom philosophy a man choosing and acting in the present is part of the unending forward surge of cosmic power. He is an active, initiating agent manipulating and bending to his purposes the subject matter he finds all about him.

Seventh, freedom of choice takes place when a man, in his role as agent cause, deliberates among open alternatives made possible by contingency and potentiality, and reaches a definite decision, not determined entirely by inheritance or environment, to do this or that.

Eighth, words such as *refraining, forbearance, self-restraint* and *regret* lose their normal meaning in the novel dialect of determinism. If determinism proves to be true, we shall have to scrap much in the existing dictionaries of the world and do a great deal of re-defining.

Ninth, from the viewpoint of ethics, law and criminal law it is difficult to understand how without freedom of choice the average man would have a sufficient sense of personal responsibility for the development of adequate moral standards, or how he could be held guilty of wrongdoing.

Tenth, the doctrine of universal and eternal determinism becomes self-refuting when we pursue its full meaning to the cases of *reductio ad absurdum* clearly implied. If our choices and actions of today were all preordained yesterday, then they were equally preordained yesteryear, at the time of the American Revolution and some five billion years ago when our planetary system was probably born. I repeat, to take another instance, that for determinism the so-called "irresistible impulse" behind crimes by the insane must hold with equal force for the actions of the sane and the virtuous.

Does the summary I have just given and my study in general indicate that I have *proved* the reality of freedom of choice? I do not make that claim. However, I do think that the over-all case against an omnivorous necessity and for free choice is a powerful one. This uniquely human capability does not constitute any departure from the ways of Nature; it stems from the most basic characteristics of the universe such as contingency, individuality, potentiality, and the agent cause always acting in the present.

The existence of freedom of choice has not prevented, and will not prevent, scientists from continuing to use their techniques to discover new if-then laws. Such laws, like all others, belong in the realm of determinism. Those working in the social and behavioral sciences will find that the recognition of free choice clarifies their problems, although admittedly its presence complicates those problems.

The question remains whether completely consistent determinists—those who both consciously believe in determinism and endeavor to put that belief into practice—are likely to conduct their lives as ethically as those who are convinced of freedom of choice. Assuming the doubtful proposition that there are "completely consistent determinists" and recognizing that any answer to this query must be speculative, I believe nevertheless that, on the whole and other things being equal, morality and a sense of individual responsibility have more meaning for persons who feel assured that free choice is real. I say this even though some of the great determinists such as Spinoza have come close to being saints.

Another question is whether a thorough-going determinist will tend to act as energetically as a man who gives credence to freedom of choice. Here it is to be remembered that all doctrines of total determinism imply the *inevitability* of every human decision. I cannot think that a man holding such a belief will exercise as much initiative and effort as an adherent of free choice. The more conscious a human being is of that portentous freedom, the better his morale will probably be and the more effective he probably will become. "The 'free-willer' tends to be aggressive in his relation to the world, treats it as something to be comprehended, manipulated and dominated. His opposite number tends rather to accept the world and events as they come." [170]

Significant evidence as to the creative role played by an awareness of freedom of choice comes from the field of psychotherapy. Professor Rogers declares: "I would be at a loss to explain the positive change which can occur in psychotherapy if I had to omit the importance of the sense of free and responsible choice on the part of my clients. I believe that this experience of freedom to choose is one of the deepest elements underlying change. . . . It is the burden of being responsible for the self one chooses to be. It is the recognition of a person that he is an emerging process, not a static end product." [171]

Speaking of the meaning of a psychological study of delinquents, Professor Rogers continues: "I began to see the significance of inner autonomy. The individual who sees himself and his situation clearly and who freely takes responsibility for that self and for that situation is a very different person from the one who is simply in the grip of outside circumstances. . . . It is clear to me that in therapy . . . commitment to purpose and to meaning in life is one of the significant elements of change. It is only when the person decides, 'I am someone; I am someone worth being; I am committed to being myself,' that change becomes possible. . . .

"So I am emboldened to say that over against this view of man as unfree, as an object, is the evidence from therapy, from subjective living, and from objective research as well, that personal freedom and responsibility have a crucial significance, that one cannot live a complete life without such personal freedom and responsibility, and that self-understanding and responsible choice make a sharp and measurable difference in the behavior of the individual." [172]

I am able to verify personally Professor Rogers' remarks. For, as I have discovered through my own inner experience, full awareness of freedom of choice brings a new sense of power and exhilaration to every aspect of living.

Furthermore, I am convinced that everyone, even the most vocal determinists, in practice decide and act to a large extent as if free choice existed. The phenomenon of men negating or neglecting in practice what they profess in theory has always been so widespread that we should not be surprised to discover its presence in the day-to-day living of those who formally adhere to the necessitarian doctrine. Jean-Paul Sartre is right when he avers: "We are not free to cease being free." [173] He is right, because freedom of choice is an inborn, indigenous, ineradicable characteristic of human beings.

Joseph Wood Krutch outlines the over-all social consequences of the vogue of determinism: "Educators, sociologists, and lawmakers have begun to act as though man were absolutely incapable of choice, of self-determination, or of any autonomous activity. . . . Moreover and merely by being treated as though he could do nothing for himself man is, perhaps, actually becoming less capable of doing so. Any society which not merely tells its members that they are automata but also treats them as though they were, runs the risk of becoming a society in which human capacities atrophy because they are less and less rewarded, or even tolerated, as well as less and less acknowledged. As the individual becomes, either in theory or in fact, less capable of doing anything for himself the question what may be *done to him* inevitably comes to seem more and more interesting." [174]

If the position I have presented in this book is sound, we must discard as untrue all systems of philosophy or religion that are fundamentally deterministic or fatalistic. By the same token those theories of history are erroneous that are based in essence on economic determinism and assert that some particular economic and political outcome for society is inevitable. For if men in general are genuinely free, it follows that groups, classes, cities and nations—all composed of human individuals—in the large likewise have freedom of choice as expressed in their collective decisions. However much individual or collective freedom may be crippled or thwarted by political tyrannies, economic institutions or cultural conditioning towards conformity, in the end, as history has demonstrated again and again, men in all likelihood will rise up to reaffirm their innate and indwelling freedom of choice.

Finally, as I complete the writing of this volume, having sifted a vast amount of evidence on both sides of the question, I feel more convinced than when I began that we men are not automatons governed by either a blind fate or an all-seeing God, but that we possess the power of free choice in charting our way through life. And we are justified in taking the existence of this most basic of all freedoms as at least *a working principle* for the ongoing career of man.

Guide to Meanings

Guide to Meanings

AGENT

An initiating cause or stimulus, either human or non-human, that acts upon relatively passive substance or subject matter. An agent can itself become subject matter for some other agent.

CHANCE

Synonym for *contingency*.

CONTINGENCY

A cosmic ultimate that is the opposite or correlative of determinism or necessity; an event that either may or may not be; more precisely, the causal intersection of two or more mutually independent and previously unrelated causal series.

COSMIC ULTIMATE

A fundamental trait of the universe as a whole, of existence as such, that is common to every event and object throughout the cosmos.

DETERMINISM

A cosmic ultimate that is the opposite and correlative of contingency, and consisting of the if-then sequences, relations or laws that exist in Nature. *Total* determinism means that such laws are all-governing throughout the universe and human life; *relative* determinism means that such laws function side by side with contingency and freedom of choice.

DETERMINIST

A person who believes in total and universal determinism.

FREEDOM OF CHOICE

The human capacity to choose freely between two or more genuine alternatives or possibilities, such choosing being always limited both by the past and by the circumstances of the immediate present.

FREE WILL

See *freedom of choice.*

HUMANISM

A comprehensive and integrated philosophy or way of life that, rejecting any belief in the supernatural, relies on reason, science and democracy in striving for the happiness, freedom and progress of all mankind.

LAW

An if-then, cause-effect sequence or if-then relation existing in Nature or in man-made machines or other devices. Such laws constitute the realm of determinism or necessity.

LIBERTARIAN

A person who believes in the existence of freedom of choice or free will.

METAPHYSICAL ULTIMATE

Synonym for *cosmic ultimate.*

METAPHYSICS

The branch of philosophy that searches out and defines the cosmic or metaphysical ultimates.

NECESSITARIAN

A person who believes that necessity rules throughout all space and time; synonym for determinist.

NECESSITY

Synonym for *determinism.*

PLURALISM

The theory that the universe is basically not a one, but a many that stems from diverse modes of being, various centers of action and multiple causes.

POTENTIALITY

A cosmic or metaphysical ultimate, meaning that every event or object in the universe has plural possibilities of action, interaction, change and development.

PREDESTINATION

Theological or Christian determinism with the accent on an omnipotent and omniscient God who preordains everything that happens, so that human individuals are predestined by Him to heaven or hell in the life after death.

SUBJECT MATTER

In the context of this book, a substance that is relatively passive and acted upon by the dynamic agent, human or non-human, in the form of efficacious cause.

UNIVERSALS

The general ideas or abstractions that are central to the process of thinking, and under which can be classified many different particulars.

Reference Notes

Reference Notes

CHAPTER 1. THE PERENNIAL DEBATE

1. *Plutarch's Morals* (Boston: Little, Brown, 1870), Vol. III, p. 129.
2. Quoted from Plutarch by Cyril Bailey, *The Greek Atomists and Epicurus* (New York: Russell & Russell, 1964), p. 120.
3. Quoted *ibid.*, p. 318.
4. Lucretius, *On the Nature of Things*, tr. by Charles E. Bennett (New York: Walter J. Black, 1946), pp. 66-67, 69.
5. William James, "The Dilemma of Determinism," *The Will to Believe and Other Essays in Popular Philosophy* (New York: Longmans, Green, 1923), p. 145.
6. John David Mabbott, "Free Will," Encyclopaedia Britannica, 1963, Vol. 9, p. 746.
7. Cicero, "On Fate," *De Oratore* (Cambridge, Mass.: Harvard University Press, 1942), Vol. II, p. 225.
8. James, *op. cit.*, p. 150.
9. Charles W. Hendel, Jr. (ed.) *Hume Selections* (New York: Scribners, 1927), p. 161.
10. Erasmus-Luther, *Discourse on Free Will* (New York: Ungar, 1961), pp. 3-4.
11. *Ibid.*, p. 106.

12. Jonathan Edwards, "Sinners in the Hands of an Angry God," *Puritan Sage: Collected Writings of Jonathan Edwards* (New York: Library Publishers, 1953), pp. 372, 375-76.

13. *A Treatise of the Faith and Practice of the Original Free Will Baptists* (Nashville: National Association of Free Will Baptists, 1962), pp. 8-9.

      See also Damon C. Dodd, *The Free Will Baptist Story* (Nashville: National Association of Free Will Baptists, 1956).

14. Thornton Wilder, *The Bridge of San Luis Rey* (New York: Albert and Charles Boni, 1928), p. 219.

15. Leo Tolstoy, *War and Peace* (New York: Simon and Schuster, 1942), p. 1336.

16. Anatole France, *A Mummer's Tale*, tr. by Charles E. Roche (New York: Gabriel Wells, 1924), p. 119.

17. Herman Melville, *Moby Dick or the Great White Whale* (Boston: Page Co., 1919), pp. 504-05, 521.

18. William Shakespeare, *Julius Caesar*, Act I, Sc. 2.

19. William Shakespeare, *King Lear*, Act I, Sc. 2.

20. Thomas Hardy, *The Dynasts, A Drama of the Napoleonic Wars* (New York & London: Macmillan, 1904), p. 87.

21. *Ibid.*, p. 2.

22. *Ibid.*, p. 103.

23. John Masefield, *Poems by John Masefield—Complete Edition with Recent Poems* (New York: Macmillan, 1953), p. 374.

24. Isaiah Berlin, *Historical Inevitability* (London: Oxford University Press, 1954), p. 74.

25. Letter from Prime Minister Nehru to the author's wife, Helen Lamb Lamont, 1952.

26. Fyodor Dostoievsky, *The Brothers Karamazov*, tr. by Constance Garnett (New York: Random House, 1933), pp. 262-264.

27. *Ibid.*, p. 264.

28. Erich Fromm, *Escape From Freedom* (New York: Avon Books, 1965), p. xii.

29. *Ibid.*, p. viii.

30. Paul Kurtz, *Humanism and Responsibility* (American Ethical Union: New York, 1967).

31. Attributed to Madame de Stael and quoted by Tolstoy, *War and Peace, op. cit.,* p. 108.

32. Edmund Bergler, *The Superego* (New York: Grune and Stratton, 1952), p. 320.

33. Dante Alighieri, *Paradise,* Canto V, verses 17 ff.

34. Milič Čapek, *The Philosophical Impact of Contemporary Physics* (Princeton: Van Nostrand, 1961), pp. 334-35.

35. James Boswell, *The Life of Samuel Johnson,* AEtat 60, Oct. 10, 1769.

36. Quoted in Paul Edwards and Arthur Pap (eds.) *A Modern Introduction to Philosophy: Readings from Classical and Contemporary Sources* (New York: Collier-Macmillan, 1966), p. 6.

37. Horace M. Kallen, "The Comic Spirit in the Freedom of Man," *Teachers College Record* (Vol. 68, No. 3, Dec. 1966), p. 187.

38. *Spinoza's Works,* tr. by R. H. M. Elwes (London: G. Bell and Sons, 1919), Letter LXII, pp. 390-91.

39. Baron d'Holbach, *Good Sense; or, Natural Ideas* (New York: G. Vale, 4th ed., 1856), pp. 51-52.

CHAPTER 2. CAN FREEDOM AND DETERMINISM CO-EXIST?

40. Viktor E. Frankl, *The Doctor and the Soul* (New York: Knopf, 1957), p. 86.

41. Horace M. Kallen, "What Is Real and What Is Illusory in Human Freedom," in Horace M. Kallen (ed.) *Freedom in the Modern World* (New York: Coward-McCann, 1928), pp. 298-99.

42. Cf. Frederick Engels: "Freedom therefore consists in the control over ourselves and over external nature which is founded on the knowledge of natural necessity." *Anti-Duhring* (New York: International Publishers), Marxist Library, Vol. XVIII, p. 131.

43. William Gruen, "Determinism, Fatalism and Historical Materialism," *Journal of Philosophy* (Nov. 5, 1939), p. 627.

44. Edwin A. Burtt, *Right Thinking: A Study of Its Principles and Methods* (New York: Harpers, 1948), p. 304.

45. Milič Čapek, "The Doctrine of Necessity Re-Examined," *Review of Metaphysics* (Sept. 1951), p. 47.

46. Charles Hartshorne, *Beyond Humanism: Essays in the New Philosophy of Nature* (Chicago, New York: Willett, Clark, 1937), pp. 148-49.

47. Sidney Hook, *The Hero in History: A Study in Limitation and Possibility* (New York: John Day, 1943), p. 19.

48. Carl A. Rogers, "Freedom and Commitment" (Yellow Springs, O.: American Humanist Assn., 1964), p. 1.

49. Joseph Wood Krutch, *The Measure of Man* (Indianapolis: Bobbs-Merrill, 1953), pp. 39-40.

50. Albert Einstein, "Science and Religion," in L. Bryson and L. Finkelstein (eds.) *Science, Philosophy and Religion: A Symposium* (New York: Conference on Science, Philosophy and Religion in Their Relation to the Democratic Way of Life, 1941), p. 213.

51. Albert Einstein, with Leopold Infeld, *The Evolution of Physics: The Growth of Ideas from Early Concepts to Relativity and Quanta* (New York: Simon and Schuster, 1938), p. 313.

CHAPTER 3. CONTINGENCY AND A PLURALISTIC WORLD

52. Aristotle, *Metaphysics,* tr. by W. D. Ross (Oxford: Oxford University Press, 1928), Gamma, Ch. 1, 1003a 21-26; Epsilon, Ch. 1, 1025b 7-10.

53. John H. Randall, Jr., *Aristotle* (New York: Columbia University Press, 1960), pp. 182-83.

54. *Ibid.,* p. 187.

55. Sterling P. Lamprecht, *Nature and History* (New York: Columbia University Press, 1950), p. 114.

56. Sterling P. Lamprecht, *The Metaphysics of Naturalism* (New York: Appleton-Century-Crofts, 1967), pp. 192-93.

57. Gardner Williams in Corliss Lamont (ed.) *A Humanist Symposium on Metaphysics* (Yellow Springs, O.: American Humanist Assn., 1960), p. 14.

58. Thomas Hardy, *The Poetical Works of Thomas Hardy* (London: Macmillan, 1920), Vol. I, p. 288.

59. *The New York Times,* Oct. 3, 1964, p. 1.

60. John H. Randall, Jr., in Lamont (ed.) *op. cit.*, pp. 19-20.

61. Two excellent books about the *Titanic* disaster are *The Truth about the Titanic* (New York: Mitchell Kennerley, 1913), by Colonel Archibald Gracie, one of the survivors; and *A Night to Remember* (New York: Bantam Books, 1956), by Walter Lord.

   I am much indebted to Rabbi Leo Shubow, my friend and classmate in the Harvard Class of 1924, for helpful suggestions about the sinking of the *Titanic*.

62. Jerome Frank, *Fate and Freedom* (New York: Simon and Schuster, 1945), p. 43.

63. Oscar Handlin, *Change or Destiny; Turning Points in American History* (Boston: Little, Brown, 1955), p. 192.

64. Cf. Ernest Nagel, "Determinism in History," *Philosophy and Phenomenological Research* (March 1960), pp. 309-10.

   Professor Nagel disagrees with Professor Handlin and me about the Battle of Yorktown.

65. J. C. Squire (ed.) *If; or, History Rewritten* (New York: Viking Press, 1931).

66. Bernhard Berenson, *Rumor and Reflection* (New York: Simon and Schuster, 1952), p. 110.

67. Berlin, *op. cit.*, p. 3.

68. *Ibid.*, p. 26.

69. *Ibid.*, p. 78.

70. *Ibid.*

71. Edward H. Carr, *What Is History?* (New York: Knopf, 1964), pp. 130, 138.

72. *Ibid.*, pp. 98-99.

73. *Ibid.*, p. 121.

74. *Ibid.*

75. Quoted by Ved Mehta, "The Flight of Crook-Taloned Birds—I," *New Yorker* (Dec. 8, 1962), p. 78.

76. Karl Marx and Frederick Engels, *The Communist Manifesto*, in *A Handbook of Marxism* (New York: Random House, 1935), p. 36.

77. Karl Marx, *Capital* (Chicago: Charles H. Kerr, 1926), Vol. I, p. 13.

78. Karl Marx, *A Contribution to the Critique of Political Economy* (Chicago: Charles H. Kerr, 1904), pp. 11-12.
79. Karl Marx and Frederick Engels, *The German Ideology* (New York: International Publishers, 1939), p. 14.
80. Karl Marx and Frederick Engels, *Correspondence, 1846-1895* (New York: International Publishers, 1935), pp. 517-18.
81. Brand Blanshard, "Can the Philosopher Influence Social Change?" *Journal of Philosophy* (Nov. 25, 1954), p. 745.
    See also Prof. Blanshard's "Reflections on Economic Determinism," *Journal of Philosophy* (March 31, 1966), and the inadequate reply, "Blanshard's Reduction of Marxism," by Dr. Ivan Babic of the University of Zagreb, *Journal of Philosophy* (Dec. 8, 1966).
82. John Dewey, "A Philosophy of Scientific Method," a review of Morris R. Cohen's *Reason and Nature* in *New Republic* (April 29, 1931), p. 307.
83. John Dewey, "Philosophies of Freedom," in Kallen (ed.) *op. cit.*, pp. 264-65.
84. George Boas, "Charles Bernard Renouvier," Encyclopedia of Philosophy, Vol. 7, p. 181.
85. William James, *A Pluralistic Universe* (New York: Longmans, Green, 1925), pp. 321-22.
86. John Dewey, "The Need for a Recovery of Philosophy," in Dewey and Others, *Creative Intelligence* (New York: Henry Holt, 1917), pp. 15-16.
87. Čapek, "The Doctrine of Necessity Re-Examined," *loc. cit.*, p. 18.
88. Quoted by Mortimer J. Adler, *The Idea of Freedom: A Dialectical Examination of the Conceptions of Freedom* (Garden City, N.Y.: Doubleday, 1958), p. 450.
89. Pierre Simon Laplace, *Oevres Complètes de Laplace* (Paris: Government of France, 1886), Vol. VII, p. 6.
90. I am grateful to attorney Harrington Harlow for providing information about the law in relation to "Acts of God."
91. Čapek, *The Philosophical Impact of Contemporary Physics*, *op. cit.*, p. 311.
92. Donald C. Williams, "Free Will or Freedom of the Will," Encyclopedia Americana, 1957, Vol. XII, p. 46.

93. Alfred Landé, "The Case for Indeterminism," in Sidney Hook (ed.) *Determinism and Freedom in the Age of Modern Science* (New York: New York University Press, 1958), p. 70.
94. *Ibid.*

CHAPTER 4. THE ROLE OF POTENTIALITY AND DELIBERATION

95. Frederick J. E. Woodbridge, *Nature and Mind* (New York: Columbia University Press, 1937), p. 52.
96. Lamprecht, *The Metaphysics of Naturalism, op. cit.*, pp. 192-193.
97. *Ibid.*, p. 193.
98. Alfred N. Whitehead, *Adventures of Ideas* (New York: Macmillan, 1933), p. 356.
99. George H. Mead, *Mind, Self and Society* (Chicago: University of Chicago Press, 1954), p. 98.
100. Dewey, "Philosophies of Freedom," *op. cit.*, pp. 240, 243, 266.
101. Charles Hartshorne, *The Logic of Perfection and Other Essays in Neoclassical Metaphysics* (La Salle, Ill.: Open Court, 1962), p. 170.
102. Hartshorne, *Beyond Humanism, op. cit.*, p. 134.
103. Keith Lehrer, "Can We Know that We Have Free Will by Introspection?" *Journal of Philosophy* (March 1, 1960), p. 145.
104. Dewey, "Philosophies of Freedom," *op. cit.*, p. 256.
105. Frankl, *op. cit.*, p. 86.
106. Viktor E. Frankl, *Man's Search for Meaning* (New York: Washington Square Press, 1959), pp. 104-05.
107. Mabbott, *op. cit.*, p. 747.
108. Gardner Williams, "Human Freedom and the Uniformity of Nature," *The Humanist* (Winter 1948-49), p. 180.
109. Frank, *op. cit.*, pp. 321-22.
110. *Ibid.*, p. 322.
111. Abraham Wolf, "Free-Will," Encyclopaedia Britannica (Fourteenth Ed., 1929), Vol. 9, p. 747.
112. Quoted by Adler, *op. cit.*, Vol. II, p. 454.

113. Quoted, *ibid.*, p. 456.
114. Paul Weiss, *Nature and Man* (New York: Holt, 1947), p. 26.
115. *Ibid.*, pp. 24, 26.
116. Carl R. Rogers, *On Becoming a Person: A Therapist's View of Psychotherapy* (Boston: Houghton Mifflin, 1961), pp. 391-92.
117. Raphael Demos, "Human Freedom—Negative and Positive," in Ruth Nanda Anshen (ed.) *Freedom: Its Meaning* (New York: Harcourt, Brace, 1940), pp. 600-01.
118. F. C. S. Schiller, *Studies in Humanism* (London: Macmillan, 1912), p. 404.
119. *Ibid.*
120. See Roberto Zavalloni, *Self-Determination: The Psychology of Personal Freedom* (Chicago: Forum Books, 1962), p. 227.
121. Paul Weiss, "Common Sense and Beyond," in Hook (ed.) *op. cit.*, p. 220.

CHAPTER 5. CAUSATION AND FREE CHOICE

122. Čapek, "The Doctrine of Necessity Re-Examined," *loc. cit.*, pp. 50-51.
123. Frederick J. E. Woodbridge, *The Purpose of History* (New York: Columbia University Press, 1916), pp. 5, 40, 47.
124. *Ibid.*, pp. 35-36, 38-39.
125. Lamprecht, *The Metaphysics of Naturalism*, *op. cit.*, pp. 149-50.
126. James, "The Dilemma of Determinism," *op. cit.*, p. 155.
127. John Dewey, *The Quest for Certainty* (New York: Minton, Balch, 1929), pp. 249-50.
128. Randall in Lamont (ed.) *op. cit.*, p. 21.
129. Hartshorne, *The Logic of Perfection*, *op. cit.*, pp. 162-64.
130. Čapek, "The Doctrine of Necessity Re-Examined," *loc. cit.*, p. 49.
131. Milič Čapek, "Toward a Widening of the Notion of Causality," *Diogenes* (Winter, 1959), p. 88.
132. Hartshorne, *The Logic of Perfection*, *op. cit.*, p. 186.

133. Wm. Pepperell Montague, "Free Will and Fate," *The Personalist* (Spring, 1943), p. 175.

134. Paul Kurtz, *Decision and the Condition of Man* (Seattle: University of Washington Press, 1965), p. 241.

135. Dewey, "Philosophies of Freedom," *op. cit.*, p. 266.

136. Barrows Dunham, *Heroes and Heretics* (New York: Knopf, 1964), p. 20.

137. Adler, *op. cit.*, Vol. II, p. 362.

138. John Macmurray, *The Self as Agent* (London: Faber and Faber, 1957), pp. 135, 139.

139. Čapek, "The Doctrine of Necessity Re-Examined," *loc. cit.*, p. 40.

CHAPTER 6. SOME PRACTICAL PROBLEMS

140. James, "The Dilemma of Determinism," *op. cit.*, p. 157.

141. Wilfrid Sellars, "Fatalism and Determinism," in Keith Lehrer (ed.) *Freedom and Determinism* (New York: Random House, 1966), pp. 146, 149.

142. Hartshorne, *Beyond Humanism, op. cit.*, p. 155.

143. John Dewey, *Reconstruction in Philosophy* (New York: Holt, 1920), p. 176.

144. Austin Farrer, *The Freedom of the Will* (New York: Scribners, 1960), p. 232.

145. Lehrer (ed.) *op. cit.*, pp. 45-63.

146. *Ibid.*, pp. 62-63.

147. Berlin, *op. cit.*, pp. 75, 31.

148. Demos, *op. cit.*, p. 590.

149. Rom. VII, 19.

150. Adler, *op. cit.*, Vol. II, p. 314.

151. C. A. Campbell, *In Defence of Free Will, With Other Philosophical Essays* (London: Allen & Unwin, 1967), p. 23.

152. James, *op. cit.*, pp. 159-60.

153. *Ibid.*, pp. 163, 175-76.

154. *Ibid.*, pp. 161-62.

155. A. E. Housman, *Last Poems* (New York: Holt, 1934), pp. 33-34.

156. *Plea of Clarence Darrow in Defense of Richard Loeb and*

Nathan Leopold Jr. on Trial for Murder (Chicago: Ralph Fletcher Seymour, 1924), pp. 29-30.

157. David L. Bazelon, *Civil Liberties in New York* (New York: New York Civil Liberties Union, April 1966), p. 5.

158. Encyclopaedia of the Social Sciences (New York: Macmillan, 1932), IV, Vol. Eight, p. 65.

159. *The New York Times*, March 1, 1966, p. 1.

160. *Ibid.*, p. 21.

161. Mabbott, *op. cit.*, p. 749.

162. B. F. Skinner, *Walden Two* (New York: Macmillan Paperbacks, 1962), p. 292.

163. *Ibid.*, p. 262.

164. *Ibid.*, p. 257.

165. B. F. Skinner, *Science and Human Behavior* (New York: Macmillan, 1953), pp. 447-48.

166. Rogers, *On Becoming a Person, op. cit.*, p. 391.

167. *Ibid.*, p. 392.

168. John Hospers, "Free Will and Psychoanalysis," in Edwards and Pap (eds.) *op. cit.*, p. 78.

169. *Ibid.*, p. 82.

CHAPTER 7. SUMMARY AND CONCLUSION

170. Allan M. Munn, *Free Will and Determinism* (Toronto: University of Toronto Press, 1960), p. 214.

171. Rogers, "Freedom and Commitment," *loc. cit.*, pp. 6-7.

172. *Ibid.*, pp. 9, 11.

173. Jean-Paul Sartre, *Being and Nothingness* (New York: Washington Square Press, 1966), p. 537.

174. Krutch, *op. cit.*, p. 40.

Selected Bibliography

Selected Bibliography

Adler, Mortimer J. *The Idea of Freedom: A Dialectical Examination of the Conceptions of Freedom.* Garden City, N. Y.: Doubleday, 1958.

Anshen, Ruth Nanda (ed.). *Freedom: Its Meaning.* New York: Harcourt, Brace, 1940.

Aristotle. *Metaphysics.*

Bergson, Henri. *Time and Free Will: An Essay on the Immediate Data of Consciousness.* New York: Harpers, 1960.

Berlin, Isaiah. *Historical Inevitability.* London: Oxford University Press, 1954.

Bunge, Mario. *Causality: The Place of the Causal Principle in Modern Science.* Cleveland and New York: World, 1963.

Berofsky, Bernard (ed.). *Free Will and Determinism.* New York: Harpers, 1966.

Blanshard, Brand. "Reflections on Economic Determinism," *The Journal of Philosophy.* March 31, 1966.

Campbell, C. A. *In Defence of Free Will, With Other Philosophical Essays.* London: Allen & Unwin, 1967.

Čapek, Milič. *The Philosophical Impact of Contemporary Physics.* Princeton: Van Nostrand, 1961.

———. "The Doctrine of Necessity Re-Examined," *The Review of Metaphysics.* Vol. X, No. 1, Sept. 1951.

SELECTED BIBLIOGRAPHY

Carr, Edward H. *What Is History?* New York: Knopf, 1964.

Cohen, Chapman. *Determinism or Free-Will?* London: Pioneer Press, 1919.

Darrow, Clarence. *Plea in Defense of Richard Loeb and Nathan Leopold Jr. on Trial for Murder.* Chicago: Ralph Fletcher Seymour, 1924.

Davidson, M. *The Free Will Controversy.* London: Watts & Co., 1942.

Dewey, John. "Philosophies of Freedom," in Horace M. Kallen (ed.) *Freedom in the Modern World.* New York: Coward-McCann, 1928.

Edwards, Jonathan. *Freedom of the Will.* Paul Ramsey (ed.). New Haven: Yale University Press, 1957.

Encyclopedia of Philosophy, The. Paul Edwards (editor-in-chief). New York: Macmillan & Free Press, 1967.

Erasmus-Luther. *Discourse on Free Will.* New York: Ungar, 1961.

Farrer, Austin. *Freedom of the Will.* New York: Scribners, 1960.

Frank, Jerome. *Fate and Freedom.* New York: Simon and Schuster, 1945.

Frankl, Viktor E. *Man's Search for Meaning.* New York: Washington Square Press, 1959.

Fromm, Erich. *Escape from Freedom.* New York: Avon Books, 1965.

Hartshorne, Charles. *The Logic of Perfection and Other Essays in Neoclassical Metaphysics.* La Salle, Ill.: Open Court, 1962.

Hook, Sidney (ed.). *Determinism and Freedom in the Age of Modern Science.* New York: New York University Press, 1958.

James, William. "The Dilemma of Determinism," in *The Will to Believe and Other Essays in Popular Philosophy.* New York: Longmans, Green, 1923.

Kallen, Horace M. (ed.). *Freedom in the Modern World.* New York: Coward-McCann, 1928.

Krutch, Joseph Wood. *The Measure of Man.* Indianapolis: Bobbs-Merrill, 1953.

Kurtz, Paul. *Decision and the Condition of Man.* Seattle: University of Washington Press, 1965.

Lamont, Corliss (ed.). *A Humanist Symposium on Metaphysics.* Yellow Springs, O.: American Humanist Association, 1960.

Lamprecht, Sterling P. *Nature and History.* New York: Columbia University Press, 1950.

————. *The Metaphysics of Naturalism.* New York: Appleton-Century-Crofts, 1967.

Lehrer, Keith (ed.). *Freedom and Determinism.* New York: Random House, 1966.

Marx, Karl, and Engels, Frederick, in *A Handbook of Marxism.* New York: Random House, 1935.

————. *Correspondence, 1846-1895.* New York: International Publishers, 1935.

Popper, Karl R. *The Open Society and Its Enemies.* New York: Harper & Row, 1963.

Randall, John Herman, Jr. *Aristotle.* New York: Columbia University Press, 1960.

Rogers, Carl R. *On Becoming a Person: A Therapist's View of Psychotherapy.* Boston: Houghton Mifflin, 1961.

Sartre, Jean-Paul. *Being and Nothingness.* New York: Washington Square Press, 1966.

Schopenhauer, Arthur. *Essay on the Freedom of the Will.* New York: Liberal Arts Press, 1960.

Skinner, B. F. *Walden Two.* New York: Macmillan, 1948.

Squire, J. C. (ed.). *If; or, History Rewritten.* New York: Viking Press, 1931.

Weiss, Paul. *Nature and Man.* New York: Holt, 1947.

————. *Man's Freedom.* New Haven: Yale University Press, 1950.

Woodbridge, Frederick J. E. *The Purpose of History.* New York: Columbia University Press, 1916.

Zavalloni, Roberto. *Self-Determination: The Psychology of Personal Freedom.* Chicago: Forum Books, 1962.

Index

Index

Books Edited by Corliss Lamont

Dialogue on John Dewey, Horizon Press, New York, NY, 1981. (Write Author)

Dialogue on George Santayana, Horizon Press, New York, NY, 1981. (Write Author)

Man Answers Death, Philosophical Library, New York, NY, 1954.

Collected Poems of John Reed, Lawrence Hill Books, Brooklyn, NY, 1985.

The Trial of Elizabeth Gurley Flynn by the American Civil Liberties Union, Horizon Press, New York, NY, 1969.